INDIANS ON HORSEBACK

INDIANS ON HORSEBACK

by ALICE MARRIOTT

Drawings by Margaret Lefranc

THOMAS Y. CROWELL COMPANY
NEW YORK

By the Author

WINTER-TELLING STORIES

INDIANS ON HORSEBACK

INDIANS OF THE FOUR CORNERS

For Adults

THE TEN GRANDMOTHERS

MARIA, THE POTTER OF SAN ILDEFONSO

THE VALLEY BELOW

THESE ARE THE PEOPLE

FOURTH PRINTING

Manufactured in the United States of America by the Vail-Ballou Press, Inc., Binghamton, New York

For MOLLY
because we went to Gallup

CONTENTS

1

WHO THE PLAINS INDIANS ARE

/\

THE FIRST HOME of the Plains Indians probably was on the plains, or steppes, of Siberia and northern Asia. There they fished and hunted and traveled, moving eastward little by little, till they came to the shores of a great sea. A long hook of rock stuck out from the mainland, stretching out across the water as far as the people could see. There was game on the land and there were fish in the ocean, so the people moved out on the land hook, still fishing and hunting and traveling.

In summer, this new land that they were crossing very slowly and through many years, was covered with short grass and small flowers. There were few bushes and no trees, but the travelers could have found driftwood that had washed ashore where they were fishing. From the driftwood the people probably built fires for cooking and to keep themselves warm.

The sea froze over in winter, and both fish and land

game were scarce in the cold weather. Maybe some of the men learned to fish through holes in the ice, but those who went hunting must have found little game. So the people moved on as quickly as they could, still going forward, since they had come too far now to turn back. In time the land broadened out before them, and the people found themselves in Alaska, and on the new continent of North America.

All this traveling happened a long time ago. Some scientists say that it was as long ago as twenty thousand years. At least it all happened before the continent of North America was completely formed, and at the time when it was still settling itself into shape. Not very long after the people had journeyed over the land bridge from Siberia, across what we call the Bering Sea, the hook-shaped bridge sank into the ocean, and the travelers were cut off from their old homes in Asia.

When these people first crossed to North America, they all did things in much the same ways. They all fished and hunted, and they all used fire. They all made ropes and cords by twisting strands of bark or sinew fiber together. They all hunted with spears; and they all had tame dogs, probably to help them with the hunting. We know that these people did these things because all the Indians in

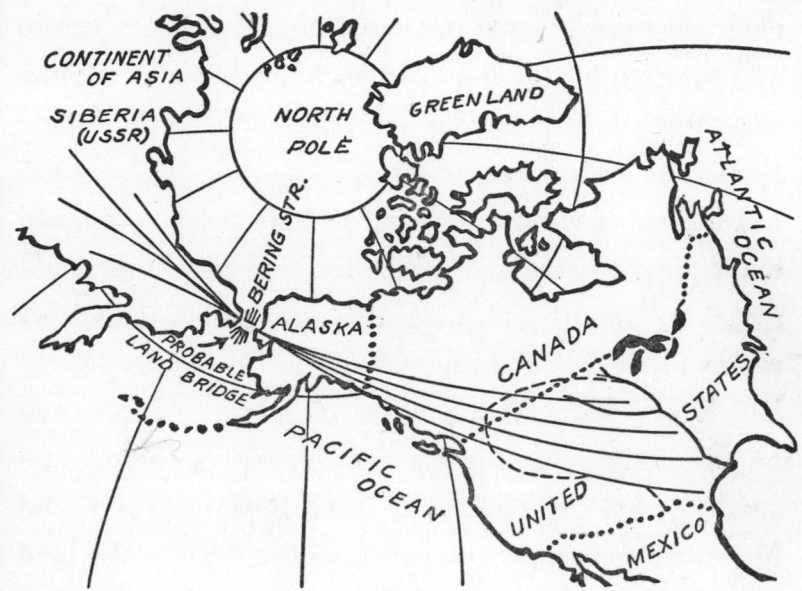

North and South America have always done them. They cannot remember a time when their tribes lacked these customs and possessions.

So far as we know, these travelers were the first people to come to North America, and they found no one there before them. After they were all alone in the new land, the people began to separate into groups of families and friends. They did not form big groups, because it was still hard for them to find food. Many people living close together could use up the fish and game quickly. As they had done before, the new family groups hunted and traveled and fished. Game was most plentiful in the south, and the country there was open. So, because it was the easiest way to go, they moved southward, on the inland side of the coastal mountains.

In time, they came to a place where the land opened out to the south and east of them, and, as far as they could see, there was an open space like an ocean of land. This was the Great Plains, where the land rolls like waves or lies flat like calm water; where there are few trees and no mountains to break the earth's surface. Rivers and streams cross the plains, but even the Mississippi and Missouri look small compared to the size of the land around them.

There they stood, those little groups of families. They looked out at the great sweep of prairie and were afraid to step onto it, for they had no way of telling what it held

or where it ended. So the people camped and made settlements along the edges of the plains, and after a time hunting parties dared to go out onto the sea of grass. Once the hunters were out upon its surface, they found the biggest animal they had ever known. This was the bison, or American buffalo. A full-grown animal weighed as much as half a ton, and had enough good meat on its bones to feed a hungry family for a long time.

This, then, was good country for the hunters. The people built their camps as near the streams as they could. Some of them learned to make small houses out of willow or cottonwood branches, and some of them used the skins of the buffalo they killed to make cone-shaped tents. The people who lived near the big Missouri River made boats

out of the buffalo skins, so that they could travel on the river. All the Indians, when they wanted to travel overland, tied poles to the backs of their dogs, letting the ends of the poles drag on the ground. Then the people piled their tents and clothes and household goods on racks tied between the poles. Because it is easier to drag a load than to carry it, the dogs were able to take the heaviest burdens, leaving the men free to hunt and the women able to care for their children while they traveled.

All these changes had taken a long time to happen. Most of the twenty thousand years were gone by now, and it was 1540 in our way of reckoning time. Away and away to the south other strangers had come to the conti-

nent. This time they came from the east. These men were the Spanish. Unlike the Indians, they came planning to settle in one place in the new country. They brought with them many of the things they were used to living with at home in Spain.

The most important and most wonderful things the Spaniards brought, to the Indians' eyes, were their horses. These were animals almost as big and strong as the buffalo, and faster running. On the backs of the horses rode the soldiers in armor, and when the Indians first saw a man dismount, they thought the animal had split itself in two. That made the new animals seem even more wonderful than the Indians had first thought them to be. In time, the Indians learned that the riders were men like themselves. Soon many of the Indians began to believe that if they had horses they, too, could ride.

It took a long time for the Indians to get horses from the Spaniards. A few of the horses were bought for painted hides, and dried meat, and tools and weapons which the Spanish needed. Some of the horses ran away from their owners, and the Indians caught them and kept them. Some of the Indians wanted horses so badly that they crept at night into the Spanish camps and took the horses away with them. In all these ways the Indians were able to get what they called "the wonderful big dogs."

Then all of a sudden a strange thing happened. The Indians found that they were no longer afraid of the great oceanlike grassland on whose edges they lived. The Indians themselves could ride out across the prairies, high enough, when they were on horseback, to see over the tall grasses and to find the buffalo herds that were still far away. It was like finding another new continent; it was like being set free. With this discovery, that they could move around easily on horseback, the Indians began a new way of life.

The Indians soon found out, too, that there were many more buffalo on the plains than they had thought. There was one great herd in the northern plains and another in the south. The herds moved from place to place, looking for fresh grass and clear water, and there were so many buffalo in each herd that it took them many days to pass a single place. With their horses, the Indians could follow the buffalo herds. They could be sure of getting meat whenever they needed it, instead of having to chance hunting without getting any game.

Not all of the Indian tribes dared to make the adventure of living out on the plains. Along the northern edges of the grasslands there still lived the Dog Knives and the

Babiche and the Tanaina; in the east were the Sauk and the Fox, the Winnebago and the Pottawatomie. Along the western edge of the plains were the Navajo and the Pueblos and the Paviotso; and in the south were the Kichai and the Tawakoni and the Wichita. None of these tribes tried the new kind of life. There were many others, too, who continued to live as they had before, but it would make too long a list to name them all.

But these are the names of some of the tribes who began the new way of living as soon as they got horses: the Cheyenne and the Arapaho; the Mandan, the Hidatsa and the Ute; the Crow and the Shoshoni; the Sioux, or Dakota; the Kiowa and the Comanche and the Jicarilla Apache; the Blackfeet and the Flatheads and the Piegan. Everyone of these tribes had its own different language, as well as its own special name.

Then the tribes who went out on the plains began to think of their whole lives in terms of moving. They had horses, so they could travel quickly and easily. They had horses, and the horses could carry heavier burdens than dogs. They had horses, so they could find, and outrun, and kill, much game.

All this meant that these Indians gave up or threw away whatever they had that was heavy or hard to take

with them on their horses. They no longer built shelters
out of brush and tree limbs, but all of them learned to
make light tents, or teepees, out of buffalo hides. Some
of the tribes, such as the Cheyenne and the Hidatsa, who
had once made baskets and pottery, stopped working at
these crafts. Like the other plains people, they learned
to make all their containers out of skins. All their clothing was made of skins, too, for weaving took a long time,
and weaving-frames were hard to carry with them.

Thus these tribes became what we call the Plains Indians; hunters, who sometimes fought each other fiercely
over the buffalo herds, and who made a game of raiding
each others' horses. Because they were hunters and fight-
ers they became fine weapon makers. Their bows and
arrows were short in order to be more easily used
on horseback. The Plains tribes made short throwing
and thrusting spears too, with which a man on horseback
could strike quickly and surely.

But the Plains Indians did not fight chiefly to
kill. They fought to defend their lands; to drive out
intruders; and to show their personal bravery. They
thought it took greater courage to touch an armed man
than to kill him, and the man who most often touched
his enemies with his bare hand or his short spear,

in battle, was considered the bravest in his group or tribe. War was like a game to the Plains Indians; not like a battle as we think of battles.

Their lives were not all made up of hunting and fighting. When there were no enemies around, and there was food enough in the teepee for everyone to eat, the men had time to make religious songs and ceremonies. Some of these songs are still sung; and some of the ceremonies are still performed. Women took part in a few of the ceremonies, which were really long prayers in the form of dances and songs.

Most of the time, though, the women were busy with other work. The women tanned the hides that the men brought home from hunting, and cut and sewed teepees and clothing from the tanned skins. They made moccasins for foot covering, and painted designs on them with earth colors. They dried the buffalo meat and then pounded it with stone hammers. The finely powdered meat they mixed with fat and berries and stored away for winter use. The women did not work as hard at any one time as the men did when they were hunting, but the women's work went on steadily every day.

The children learned to do as their elders did, for most of their games were imitation work. They played camping and hunting and fighting; and the little girls played with dolls and at keeping house. There were other games, too. The children slid on the ice, or skated on it with skates made of buffalo rib bones, in the winter. Sometimes they made cats' cradles of string, when the weather was too cold for them to go outdoors.

Old men and women were the rememberers of their tribes. They kept the history of what had happened in their minds, usually, for they had no way of writing. Sometimes, though, the old men drew pictures of the histories on hides, as reminders of the things that had happened and the way the events took place. And the old people remembered, too, and told to the children long stories and legends about gods and spirits and tribal heroes. All the stories were important to everybody, but only the old people had time enough to think a great deal about them.

2

WHAT THE GREAT PLAINS ARE

/\

A CONTINENT actually is made like a saucer. It is turned up, with mountains around its edges; and in the middle it is lower and almost flat. All continents have this same kind of shape, and North America is no exception. Its east and west rims are the Appalachian and the Rocky mountains, while in the middle it slopes downward to a center called the Great Plains.

We usually think of plains as flat areas, although they are not really flat. The surface of the plain curves with the curve of the earth. When you stand in the middle of this space, there is a circle of sky all around you, and you seem to be standing on a little rise. Whether you move north or south or east or west, if you are in the true Great Plains, the place where you stop will always seem to be a little higher than the land around you.

But the great surface of this earth curve is not actually

smooth. It is cut through by rivers, which dig their beds lower than the country around them. Where there had been rivers and lakes formed by these rivers in times past, the earth is low. On the banks of the rivers and the shores of the long-ago lakes the ground is high.

Where the earth is bare, the wind and the rain cut it up into hills with sharp, almost straight, sides. These hills are called bluffs. Where the bluffs are left standing alone, the wind and rain cut more deeply into their sides, and buttes and mesas are formed. To look at a plain from near by is to see all these shapes which time and the weather have left, and to wonder how the plains ever came to be called flat.

Away from the rivers and the trees that grow on their banks, the plains are usually covered with grass. Sometimes this is short grass, but it may grow to be "knee high to a man on a horse," as the cowboys used to say. As long as the grass cover grows, the plains look flatter than they really are, for the grass evens off little surface bumps and hollows, and holds the soil in place.

When the grass is plowed up and the soil of the plains is broken, water runs along the lower places during the rains, and in the dry seasons the wind runs along them like the water. Both water and wind cut away the soil, so

that more and more the plains are broken up, and more
and more of their surface looks like the ground along the
rivers and beside the old lakes. New rivers and lakes form
in the new low places, and as their banks grow higher
and higher, new bluffs and buttes are made. All these
things are going on today. The Great Plains are always
changing, like a great ocean.

The Great Plains of North America start almost at the
Arctic Circle. They stretch south through central
Canada, and on south, between the Rocky Mountains
and the Mississippi River, into Mexico. Almost a third
of the United States lies within the Great Plains area.
Our plains states are Nebraska, the two Dakotas, Minne-
sota, Montana, Wyoming, Iowa, Illinois, Indiana, Mis-

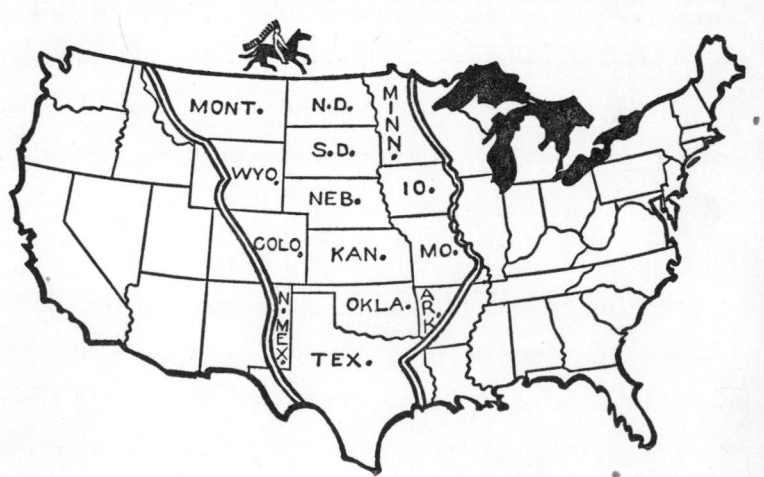

souri, Kansas, Arkansas, Oklahoma, and Texas. These are some of the biggest states, as a group, in the Union, and they make up a great stretch of country that is one or the finest places in the world for growing grain and raising cattle.

The climate of the Great Plains varies a good deal. The coldest place in the United States is in northern North Dakota. There the temperature sometimes drops to as low as 50 degrees below zero in the winter. The highest temperature ever recorded in southern Texas was 130 degrees above zero, in summer. In between these two states are places with moderate temperatures all the year round, and sections where the temperature rises and falls a great deal during the year.

The rainfall of the plains varies less than the temperature does. Generally speaking, the plains area has spring and fall rains, and some winter snow. In summer the weather is usually dry. It is this alternation of wet and dry seasons during the year that makes grain crops easy to raise.

This is the weather of average years. In some years the rains do not fall, and then, especially in the western plains, there are long periods of droughts and dust storms. In other years, the rains fall too heavily. Then there are heavy floods, especially in the eastern plains. Both droughts and floods are destructive, not only to growing crops, but to the land itself. The wind and the rain cut deep into the soil and carry it away, hurrying the formation of buttes and mesas where once there were flat areas.

Nowadays, many of the people of the plains are white men, whose ancestors came to this country from Europe. Most of them came from the northern European countries: Sweden and Denmark and Norway; Belgium and Germany; England and Ireland and Scotland. They came looking for rich soil where their crops could grow, and where they could support themselves and their families.

They came to the new land, hard workers from hard countries, knowing that here they would have to work hard, too. They built cities and schools and churches and colleges; they have earned what they have and they are proud of what they have built.

Long before these white people came, the other peoples moved into the plains from Asia, to the west. They, too, made a way of life of which they were proud and which they loved. It is their story that this book is going to tell.

3

WHEN THE WHITE MEN CAME

WWWWWWWWWWWWWWWWWWWWWWWWWW

WHILE THE LIFE of the Indians was changing, and the tribes were moving onto the plains, the white men's life was changing, too. More and more white people came into the plains country after about 1850. When they looked at the great flat prairies, the white men thought of the grasslands as places to grow corn and wheat and other grains. The newcomers began to root up the prairie grasses and plow up the earth so that they might plant their crops. So that the planted fields could grow, the white men drove away the buffalo, and fenced their lands to keep out the wild animals. When the buffalo came back to graze on the young grain, the white men killed the big animals to protect their lands and crops.

So that they could move about in the new country, the white men began building railroads across the plains. Soon they learned that the buffalo interfered with railroad traffic as much as they did with the crops. Sometimes a train had to wait for four days until one of the great buffalo herds had passed a certain place. In order that the trains could go through, the white men hired buffalo hunters to shoot the herds.

The hunters went to work in 1870, and by 1872 the two great buffalo herds were almost gone. Their hides were piled higher than the eaves of the railroad stations, where they were stored to be shipped east and made into shoe leather in Boston and other cities. The bones of the buffalo lay drying on the prairies, covering miles of country, and looking as if snow had fallen there in midsummer. So quickly were the herds wiped out that the Indians could not believe that the buffalo had been killed by men. To explain what had happened, the Plains Indians told each other that the buffalo had gone underground, and would hide there till all the white men were gone. Someday, the Indians said, the buffalo would come back, and life on the plains would be again as it was before.

These were hard times for the Plains Indians. The buffalo were what they lived on. Without the buffalo, the Indians starved and suffered. To protect their own and their children's lives, the Plains Indians tried to drive the white men away. But the white people did not fight like the Indians. The whites, too, were fighting to protect their lives and their way of living them, and they fought to kill.

Because the white settlers had guns, which were better weapons than bows and arrows, they finally won. After 1870, the white soldiers began to shut the Indians up on small areas of land, called reservations, and to hold them there. There was little food for the Indians to eat, and they had no room to go hunting. Even if they could have gone, there was almost no game left for them to bring home. Until the Plains Indians had learned to live on a small plot of land apiece, like the white farmers, they could hardly live at all. They had to give up many of their songs and ceremonies. The Indian children no longer played games, for the games they had known had no meaning any more. All the Indian life was changed.

It is of the times when the Indians were still living in their old way, before the white people settled on the plains in the 1800's, that we are going to talk now.

4

ONE MAN'S LIFE ON THE PLAINS

∧∧∧∧∧∧∧∧∧∧∧∧∧∧∧∧∧∧∧∧∧∧∧∧∧∧∧∧∧∧

IN THE EARLY DAYS, when a Plains Indian baby was born, his grandmother was usually the first person to take care of him. She took the baby and rubbed him all over with warm, melted fat from a deer or from a buffalo cow. This was to make the baby's skin soft and smooth. It kept him clean, too, as soap does. Next the grandmother wrapped the baby in little, soft-tanned rabbit or squirrel skins, and then she put him in his cradle.

Some Plains Indian tribes had two kinds of cradles. The first kind, into which the new baby was put, and where most babies slept at night until they were about two years old, was very simple. This cradle was just a tube of buffalo hide, not worked and rubbed, or tanned, to make it soft; but sun dried, so it would be stiff. Hide prepared in this way was called rawhide. It had an unfinished surface that felt a little like blotting paper, and it took paints made of earth colors easily. The women painted sharp-edged designs, like diamonds and triangles, on the cradles with blue and red and yellow earths.

The second kind of cradle was harder to make. First, the grandmother whittled out flat boards, of bois d'arc or of cedar wood. The whittling took a long time because the only tool the old lady had was a knife. When the boards were flat and smooth, the grandmother pointed their top ends and rounded off the bottom ones. Then the finished boards were about three and a half feet long, four inches wide, and half an inch thick.

Next, the grandmother made a bag, or case, of soft-tanned deer hide. She bent a curved piece of buffalo rawhide across the top of the cradle, from one board to the other. Then she stretched the soft skin bag over the boards and the rawhide. She tied the bag tightly at the bottom, where the baby's feet would rest. She fastened the case to the back boards with rawhide strings. Last of all, she lined the case with small, soft skins and laid the baby inside. She covered him over with other soft little hides, instead of with sheets and blankets.

This was a good cradle. It was made in this way so that the baby would always be safe, even if the cradle were accidentally dropped or fell when the mother was busy.

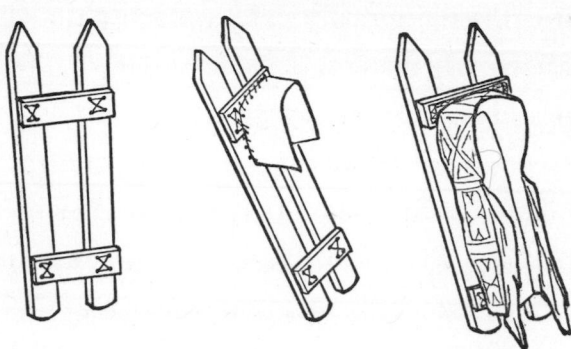

If the cradle, with the baby in it, fell headfirst, even from a horse, the sharply pointed ends of the boards would stick in the ground and hold there. The baby would be upside down, and he would probably yell, but he would be safe and unhurt. If the cradle fell feet first, it would rock back and forth on the curved lower ends of the boards, and finally rest on its side. If the cradle fell on its back, the boards and the soft skin mattress would protect the baby's spine; and, if the cradle fell face forward, the curved raw-hide hood would protect the baby's face. No matter what the mother was doing, riding or walking or working, she could feel sure that her baby would not be easily hurt.

A Plains Indian child spent most of his first two years in his cradle. Several times a day the baby's mother or grandmother would take him out; wash him; and rub his legs and arms with fat to keep them clean and to make

them grow straight and supple. Sometimes the father or
grandfather would take the baby out of the cradle. Then
he would hold the child on his lap, and let him stretch and
kick and grow. But during all the hours when the grown-
ups were busy, the baby was in his cradle, which was hung
from a teepee pole or tied to the horn of the mother's saddle. The baby could watch everything that went on
around him and still be safe and out of the way. Often the
baby was so comfortable and happy in his cradle that he
cried when he was taken out of it.

After the baby had learned to walk, he was taught that
there were some places where he should not go. He must
not go near the horses, or near the places where the young
men were dancing, or practicing with their bows and

Play
around
teepee

arrows. The best and safest place for a small child was inside the teepee or right in front of the doorway, and he was taught to play there until he was about four years old.

During these years, when the family traveled, the little child was tied on a bundle made of the teepee cover. The cover was tied to the teepee poles, and the whole load was fastened to the back of an old gentle mare, in the same way that smaller drags had once been fastened to the backs of the dogs. Sometimes, on a trip, the child's father would hold him in his arms on horseback, or would even put the small boy in front of him on the saddle, so the boy could get used to riding and to the feel of the horse.

When he was about six years old, a child learned to ride alone. At that age, a boy was given his first tiny bow and arrows, and a girl was given her first doll. The children played with their toys, but it was more than playing. A child was told that if he were old enough to have things of his own, he was old enough to take care of them and to use them in the right way. All the children tried to follow this good advice.

A boy was about six when he joined his first club, too. This was called the Rabbit Society, and it was for dancing

Rabbit Society Dance

and feasting and fun. All the little boys in the tribe belonged, and all of them took part in whatever their society did. Always in the summer, and sometimes during the winter months, the parents gave feasts for the boys. The children danced before they ate their dinner. When they danced, the boys hopped up and down, first on one foot and then on the other, and they flopped their hands up and down, like rabbits' ears, over their heads. The little girls danced, too. They formed a straight line behind their brothers and danced sidewise, with short steps. This was the same dancing step that the grown women used. After the dancing, the children feasted. If there were any food left over after they had eaten, the boys threw it at the girls and at each other. Sometimes all the children went home coated with meat and soup and dried berries.

A boy belonged to the Rabbit Society until he was about twelve. Then he joined another club, which was sometimes called the Herders' Society. From that time on the boy began to be grown up. He went out with the other boys, to watch the horse herds and to keep them from straying away from the main camp. If a boy's family had several horses, his parents gave him a horse of his own, so that he would learn how to take care of it. Instead of playing around camp with a toy bow and arrows, was given a real set, strong enough to shoot a deer, and was taken along when the men went hunting.

The most exciting thing that happened to a Plains Indian boy was his first buffalo hunt. He remembered it always, even after he got to be an old man.

Early in the morning, the camp announcers went about, calling out for all the men who wanted to go hunting to get food for their families to come to a certain teepee. The men came from their own teepees, each wearing nothing but a breechclout and a pair of moccasins. Buffalo hunting was hard work, and clothes could get in the men's way. Every man carried his bow and arrows, and had a strong, sharp knife tied to the belt that held up his breechclout.

When all the men were ready, the one who had been elected head of the game wardens for that hunt told them what they were to do. He told every man where to ride, and warned them all to keep quiet until they came to the buffalo herd. He talked to them like a football coach before a game. He was always particularly careful to tell the young boys not to get excited; not to ride out ahead of the grown men; and not to yell. If anyone did such things, he might scare the buffalo away. Then he would be forbidden to hunt for a long time, until he learned to behave better.

The men and boys rode out of camp, then, just at dawn. They had to get started early, for buffalo hunting was no work for a lazy man. Along the edges of the plains the earth and the sky would melt and run and be stuck together with a little bit of mist. When the sun came up, first there would be color in the sky and then shapes on the earth—the long shapes of men and horses spreading out on the grass. The men rode bareback and the horses were unshod, so there were few sounds. The only movements besides those of the horses were the signals of the game wardens.

When the hunters came to the buffalo herd, they stopped and sat still. Then the head of the game wardens brought his right hand up above his head and down straight to his side. That was the signal for the men to ride into the herd and start shooting. When the signal came, all the hunters kicked their horses forward into a gallop. The riders stretched out as far forward over the horses' heads as they could reach, and shot as hard and as fast as they knew how. Afterwards a man could tell which buffalo he had shot because his arrows were painted with his own design.

The First Buffalo Hunt

The shooting was over very quickly. Almost as soon as the hunters charged, the buffalo ran away. Only the dead and wounded animals were left. Sometimes a buffalo that had been shot but not killed would charge at a man and try to kill him. Then the man would ride away if he could, but if he could not escape, all the hunters would try to shoot that one buffalo and save the man. Afterward the hunters decided whose arrow had struck the animal first. If they couldn't agree, the game wardens divided the meat from the buffalo among all the hunters whose arrows had hit it.

The women followed when the men went hunting. When the shooting was over, the women came up with pack horses, to help with skinning and cutting up the meat. The women helped with this part of the work because they knew what they wanted to use the buffalo hides for, and how to get them off the best way for that purpose. Both men and women knew the best ways of cutting up the meat.

If a boy had shot his first buffalo in a hunt, his father cut out the tongue and gave it to him. The tongue was thought to be the best part of the meat. The boy gave the tongue to some of the older people who were not his relatives. To give something in this way was called a "give-away," and it was done in this case to teach the boy to be generous and to help those around him. The boy himself did not eat any meat from his first buffalo. This was to teach him not to be greedy, nor to want to get things for himself alone. In this way he learned to want to work for his family.

When he was fourteen or fifteen, a Plains Indian boy went on his first war raid. He did not take part in the fighting, unless he were in great danger and had to defend himself. Instead, he cooked for the older men and cared for their horses. He brought the men water and ran errands for them. All the time he was watching what the older people did and learning what to do himself, when the time came.

As we have already said, the Plains Indians did not make war primarily to kill one another. Most of the tribes went on raids to get horses or to take captives. Sometimes two tribes would fight over who should have the area where a certain buffalo herd lived. If one tribe had lost a fight with another, the men in the losing tribe sometimes went on a raid to get revenge.

The bravest thing that a Plains Indian man could do in warfare was to go into an enemy camp at night and take horses from the picket lines. It took a clever, skillful man to get past the guards who were watching the camp and to untie the horses and lead them away without rousing anybody.

It was considered almost equally brave to ride up to an enemy and touch him with your bare hand, or to strike him with a riding crop or a short stick. A man had to control his horse perfectly, and be a very fine rider, to do this.

Because it took so much courage and cunning to do these two things, men kept score of the number of times that they had been successful. If a man had a high score, he was allowed to wear a war bonnet. This was the same as being given a medal in our army. Because a man had to earn the right to wear it by being very brave, the Plains Indians looked on a war bonnet as something almost sacred. That is why, today, these Indians look down on white people, or on members of other tribes, who put on war bonnets and wear them just to show off. The Plains Indians know these people have not earned the right to wear Indian medals.

A Plains Indian boy did a very important thing, religiously, when he was about fourteen. He went out all alone, to look for a spirit guardian who would help and protect him for the rest of his life. The boy went to a high bluff or mesa that was not too far from camp. There he stayed, all alone, for four days and nights. During that whole time, the boy was not supposed to eat or drink, but to pray and wait for the spirit to come to him.

Many boys never saw the vision of a spirit guardian. Those who did not sometimes went again to look for one. Some of them gave up after the first attempt. The boys who had visions usually saw the spirits of animals, such as bears or eagles or coyotes. The animal that the boy saw gave him its own strengths and skills, and told him what he must and must not do to keep them.

A boy who had an eagle vision, for instance, was supposed to see his enemies from afar and to strike them swiftly. He must never eat eagle meat, though, or he would lose his power. At the same time, he was supposed to wear eagle feathers, so he could get extra power directly from them, whenever he needed it.

In some tribes, the boys took names that referred to their spirit guardians. A boy with an eagle guardian might call himself Strong Flier or Long Claws, or some other name that spoke of things that the eagle did.

Because these spirit visions were considered very sacred, the boys told them to no one, but kept their visions secret in their own hearts. Only very old men ever told about their visions. Then, if they wanted to share the powers given them by their spirit guardians, they told their visions to their sons or grandsons.

As the girls grew up, they were taught the ways of a woman's life. They helped their mothers in the teepees. They learned to cook and sew; to put the teepees up and to take them down again; to load and unload the pack horses that carried the household goods. The girls who were interested in such work learned to paint designs on clothing and on the rawhide cases in which they kept their belongings. The girls were taught all the things that a woman needed to know in order to take care of her family.

The girls did not join any societies or go out on war parties. Their mothers kept them close at home, and watched over them. They did go out with the older women to help with the skinning and butchering after buffalo hunts. Girls did not go out to look for visions. The only religious thing they were taught to do was to take part in some of the sacred dances.

Still the girls had a good time. Usually three or four of them worked and sewed together, with an older woman sitting near them to show them how to do things. The girls talked things over in groups. They played kickball, bouncing the rawhide balls with their feet; and stick-

game, which is a game like parcheesi. The young women, too, enjoyed these games, and played them even after they were nearly grown up.

It was not until a young man had been on several hunts and had made his first raid, so he had proved that he could bring home buffalo and horses, that he began to think about getting married. Then he knew that he could take care of himself and of a family, too. Usually he thought things over for a long time, before he made up his mind what girl he wanted to marry.

Then the young man went to his father and told him about it. If the father thought that it was all right, and that his son was old enough and wise enough to make his own home, he agreed. He gave his consent to his son's marrying.

A few days later, the boy's parents put on their best clothes and went to see the family of the girl their son had chosen. To show their respect for the girl and her people, the boy's parents took presents with them: horses, and tanned hides, and knives, and perhaps cloth that they had bought from the white traders. They did not mention their presents; they just tied the horses, loaded with the goods, outside the teepee door. Then the boy's family went inside and sat down and talked to the girl's parents. They said that their son wished to marry the other family's daughter.

When the young man's family had explained things and had gone home, the girl's parents told her about what had happened. Since she was sitting inside the teepee all the time, she naturally knew about it, but her family thought it was polite to tell her, anyway. The girl did not have to marry the young man if she did not want to. She could explain how she felt to her parents. Then they took the horses and the rest of the presents back to the young man's parents.

But if the young woman were pleased, and said so, her family kept the gifts. Then the girl's parents began getting things ready to take to the young man's family. They chose the best things they owned to give away. When ev-

A Marriage Proposal

erything had been gathered together and loaded on horseback, the girl dressed in her best clothes. Then, with her family following her, she led the horses over to the young man's teepee. His mother and sisters came out to meet the bride, and take the horses she was leading. Then the boy's relatives led the bride inside their teepee, and from that time on she was a member of that family as well as of her own.

Making the first teepee for her new home was the most exciting thing for a young woman; as exciting as the first buffalo hunt was for a young man.

All the older women gathered at the teepee of the girl's mother. A woman who was a skilled cutter cut the buffalo hides into just the right pieces with her knife.

Then all of the women worked to sew the pieces of skin together and make the teepee cover.

After that was finished, the older women gave the bride her presents. Because the teepee and all of the things that went with it belonged to the woman of the family, they gave her woman's things: teepee poles, and gourd dippers, and buckets. They gave her willow-rod beds, with hides for bed coverings, and painted rawhide cases to hold food and clothes that she wanted to store away. Some of these things, such as the teepee poles, a woman kept and used as long as she lived.

As the people grew older and their own families grew up, they spent more time at home. The older men still went hunting, but they did not go out on as many war raids as the younger ones. The older men gave good advice to the young ones; they told them what to do, and the best ways of doing these things. The old men joined separate societies of their own, and spent much of their time meeting together. Then they made plans for the hunts, and for moving camp. They became counselors rather than doers.

The older people were very much respected by the younger Plains Indians for their wisdom and good advice. Because the life of all the people was hard, and not many persons lived to be very old, the younger people took great care of those who had lived a long time. The old people were waited on by their children and grandchildren. What they said was listened to and obeyed. They, in turn, gave much thought and help to the problems of the younger ones.

When the time came for a man to die, he was greatly mourned by his family and friends. Perhaps his wife and children grieved for him so much that they gashed the skin of their arms and legs till the blood ran. Women often cut off their hair when they were in mourning for a loved one.

For a year the whole family painted their faces with ashes instead of with earth colors. They wore old, ragged clothes. They burned or buried everything that had belonged to the dead person, and gave away all their own possessions.

So that they might show their respect for a dead person, his family never spoke his name again. Instead they spoke of his relationship to someone else, saying, "My father," or, "Your brother," or "Snow Woman's husband." They tried to forget his name for all the rest of their lives.

5

HOW THE TRIBES GOVERNED
THEMSELVES

∧∨∧∨∧∨∧∨∧∨∧∨∧∨∧∨∧∨∧∨∧∨∧∨∧∨∧∨∧∨∧∨∧∨

WHEN THE INDIANS first went out on the plains, as we know, they were in families and little bands. These groups soon spread wide apart so there would be game enough for everyone. As time went on, and the people married and had children, the little bands grew and increased. In time they became nations, and were known as tribes.

Because the tribes were spread out over so much territory, each one of them came to have its own ways of doing things. They became a little different from one another; first in one way, then in many ways. Even the words that they spoke became different. We do not know what languages the Indians spoke when they first crossed the land bridge from Siberia. We do not even know whether they all spoke one language; or whether there were many tongues known among them then. We do know that as they lived apart from one another each of the tribes developed its own language, and that when the white people first met them, each Indian tribe spoke a little differently from all the others.

That was all right as long as the Indians were camping along the edges of the plains. They saw few people who did not belong to their own tribes. As soon as the Indians got horses and began moving over the grasslands, though, matters changed. Men from one tribe met those from others, and when they did, they stopped to talk.

Because their languages were different, they could not understand one another, so the men began making signs with their hands to explain what they were trying to say. As time went on, each tribe learned to make the same signs that all the others did, to represent certain thoughts. In this way, what was called "sign language" was developed. Sign language became so important to the Plains Indians that after a while people even used it in speaking to members of their own tribes. They would talk along in words, saying the same things with gestures, and not realize that they were using their hands at all.

Since each tribe had its own customs, and since they **were** so scattered over the land, each one governed itself

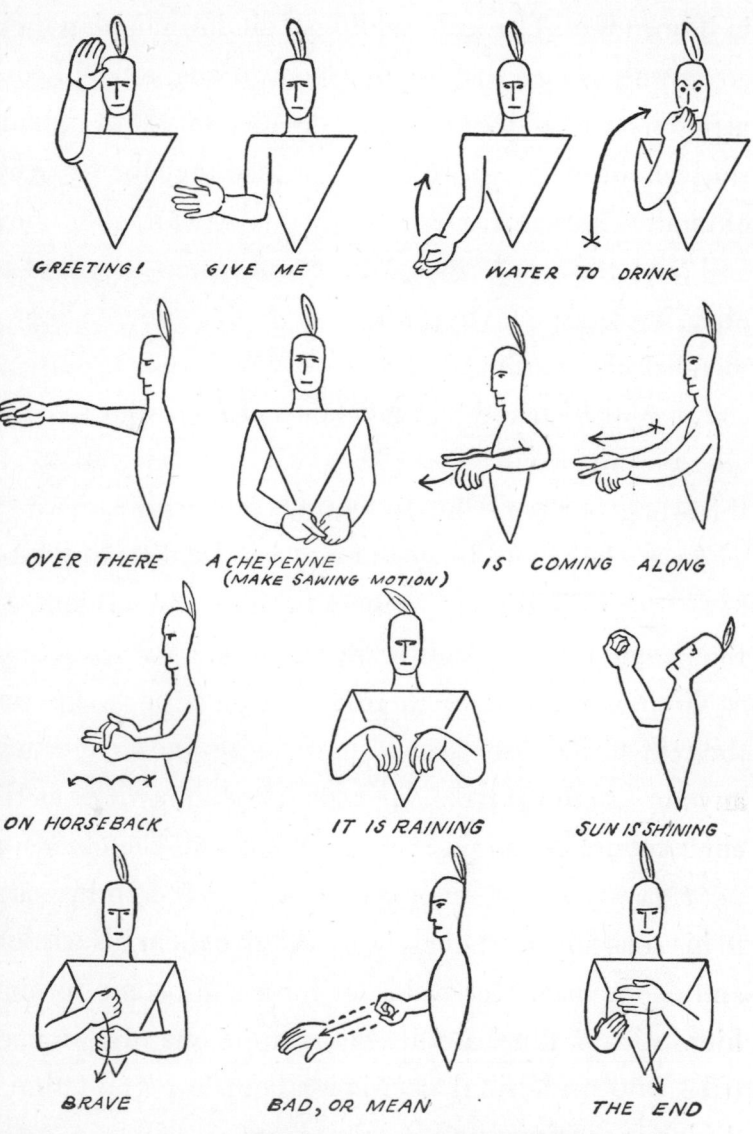

GREETING!   GIVE ME   WATER TO DRINK

OVER THERE   A CHEYENNE
(MAKE SAWING MOTION)   IS COMING ALONG

ON HORSEBACK   IT IS RAINING   SUN IS SHINING

BRAVE   BAD, OR MEAN   THE END

SIGN   LANGUAGE

in its own way. The Indians did not sit down to plan their governments and write their constitutions, or hold conventions, the way the white people do. The Indians worked out their own rules and passed them on by word of mouth. In that way everybody finally learned to know and obey the regulations. The people knew they had to obey, because staying alive depended on staying a member of the tribe.

Every tribe had a special group of men who were its advisers and counselors. They were not elected to do this work, but were chosen because they were older men who were known to be good and wise. Just because each person separately went to them for help and wisdom, all the people together did the same thing.

Of the counselors, there was always one who was thought to be wiser and to have more knowledge than anyone else in his tribe. He came to be thought of as the chief counselor or what we call the chief. The chief was not a governor or a king. He could not hand on his office to his sons any more than he could give them his wisdom and experience. He could not force the people to obey him. Still, in time, a chief became the one man in each tribe who made final decisions about important things during peace time.

Since the counselors and their chief were too old to take active part in fighting, they did not have much to do with governing their tribes during war times. Then the younger men took over, and the responsibility for caring for the people was in their hands. If the tribe were attacked, one of the men who had fought bravely in other battles became the war chief. He was not elected to his office any more than the peace chief was, but he was recognized as the leader of the tribe during the war.

If the tribe were attacking, the plan that was used was a different one. Then a man decided to go against an enemy tribe to get horses or goods, or to prove his own bravery. He called all the other men together, and told them what he wanted to do. Those who wished to might join him. If they did join, the first man went as the leader. The responsibility for the lives of the men who followed him was in his hands. That meant that the leader not only had to be brave, but also wise and skillful, so that his followers would not be in danger of being killed or hurt. When the fighting was over, the war chief was no longer head of the tribe. He was just another one of the fighting men.

Besides the chiefs and counselors, there was another group who took part in governing the tribe. These were the members of the men's societies. Sometimes, as in the buffalo hunts, the members of the societies served as game wardens. Sometimes, when the tribe was encamped and there was no hunting going on, the societies acted as camp police. Sometimes, when there was important news to be told to the people, they were the announcers.

Each society in the tribe took its turn at these duties. Sometimes it was the Kit Foxes, sometimes the Gourd Rattle Dancers, sometimes the Black-Painted Legs, or sometimes the Crazy Dogs who did the work. Usually the societies alternated, and each one knew when its turn came to serve. If one of the societies were known to be especially good at a certain kind of work, and that was the work that had to be done, then the other societies would ask that one to take charge out of turn.

In camp, it was the duty of the police to see that the teepees were pitched right, and that all the ropes and poles were firm and tight. The police instructed the people to keep their camps clean and neat, with all the rubbish picked up and burned. They told the men where to pasture their horses during the day, and where to tie the horses on the picket lines at night. It was part of the police work to see that people did not get into fights

A Member of the Crazy Dog Society with His Attendant

or quarrels with one another, and that there was no stealing. In fact, the Indian police did just the same kinds of work that our police do.

When the men went hunting, the society members were the game wardens. They kept all the men riding together, so that no one could charge ahead of the other hunters and scare off the game before everybody had had a chance to shoot. The wardens gave the signal to charge at the herd and start shooting. They told the women where to stand and how long to wait before they came up to skin the buffalo.

It was important for the Plains Indians not to kill off too much game, or to kill the buffalo cows and calves, in order to keep the herds large and growing. In that way there would always be enough meat for everybody's needs. These were the reasons it was important to have game wardens on duty in the big hunts. The wardens were so busy taking care of the herds that they had no time to get meat for their own families. The hunters shared their meat with the wardens.

When the societies were acting as camp announcers, their most important work was to tell the people when the camp was going to be moved. Then the society members rode through the camp, calling out when the tribe was going to leave; and how far they were going to travel. In that way everybody could know what the peace chief and counselors were planning for the tribe.

If a family, or one of the societies, were planning to have a great feast; or if a member of a society were going to get married; or if there were a religious ceremony to be held, the announcers told about these things, too. The same announcers told the whole camp when a man was planning to lead out a war party.

Sometimes a family would decide to have a give-away. This was like the giving away that came after a funeral, or after a boy's first hunt; but it was given for a different reason. Many times give-aways were like our birthday parties or holiday celebrations. They were given in honor of a child, or of a young man or woman.

The difference between our birthday parties and an Indian give-away is that at a give-away, instead of geting presents, the one who was holding the celebration gave gifts to other people. A family took the best things that its members had, and sometimes everything that they had, and gave the things away to people who were in need. It was very important not to give away to your own relatives, or to people who owned plenty of things of their own. One reason for having give-aways was to teach the young people to take care of those who were less fortunate than themselves, and to be generous and kind to everybody in the tribe.

Many times a family gave away all its possessions at one give-away. When they had done that, the family started in again to build up their goods. The members of the family knew that because they had shown their own generosity, other people would not let them suffer want. If a man were known to have been generous and kind to others during his own youth, he need not fear starvation in his old age. Other people, when they had their give-aways, would remember his generosity. They would take care of him then. This was not really a part of governing the tribe, but it was one of the important rules by which the members of the tribes lived and helped each other.

6

THE SUN DANCE CEREMONY

ΛΛΛΛΛΛΛΛΛΛΛΛΛΛΛΛΛΛΛΛΛΛΛΛΛΛΛΛΛ

THE BIGGEST GIVE-AWAYS held by all the Plains Indian tribes came in the middle of the summer, at the time of the Sun Dance ceremony. The Sun Dance was a great religious ceremony, which was held every year. Each of the plains tribes performed the ceremony a little differently from the others, but in some ways all the Sun Dances were pretty much alike. The one we are going to talk about here is the ceremony that was given by the Kiowa Indians, who live in the southern part of the Great Plains.

Long before the time for the ceremony came, a place to put the big camp for the dance had to be chosen. This decision was made by the man who was the religious chief of the tribe for that one dance. During the Sun Dance time, this man governed the whole tribe. It was as if one of our ministers were asked, during the Christmas season, or Easter week, to act as mayor of his city.

The Sun Dance chief made all the plans long ahead of time. He picked out a place where there would be plenty of wood for fires. There had to be lots of grass for the horses, and he made sure that there was a lot of water for everybody. Then on a certain day that he selected, the Sun Dance chief called all of the young men whom he could together. They rode out to visit all the families in the tribe, to give them word when and where the Sun Dance was to be held.

Sometimes this was a long trip. Many of the families camped away from the others, where the hunting and grazing were good. All of the families had to be notified. It might take several days to get word to all of them. But no matter how long the trip took, the Sun Dance chief and the young men who were with him rode slowly. The Plains Indians thought that you should never hurry about sacred things.

When all of the families in the tribe had been notified about the Sun Dance, they began to come to the camping place that had been chosen for it. The people pitched their teepees there. In other camps, the teepees were all set in a straight line facing east. For the Sun Dances the people camped in a big circle, with their teepees facing towards the center. A cleared place was left in the middle of the circle. There a special shelter, called the Sun Dance lodge, was to be built.

It usually took four days and nights for the whole tribe to gather together. The people felt that this length of time was just right, because in the Sun Dance everything was done by fours. The next four days, after all the tribe had met, were called "the getting-ready four days."

First, the center pole had to be cut for the lodge. Cutting the poles was a ceremonial thing that only a woman could do, and it was believed that cutting it was so sacred an act that it was dangerous. So the woman who cut the center pole was usually a captive from another tribe. The tribe did not want one of their own women to be in danger. The captive woman was dressed in her best clothes. Her face was painted yellow. She rode out of camp just behind the Sun Dance chief, on a fine horse. Behind them rode all the young men of the tribe.

When the riders came within sight of the tree that had been chosen for the center pole, the Sun Dance chief pointed to it with his whole arm. Then the young men rode forward past the chief and the captive woman, and charged at the tree as if it were an enemy. Striking the tree counted the same as striking an enemy, and the first four men to touch the center pole could count the blow as if it were a war honor.

After the young men struck the tree, the captive woman chopped it down. Then she painted four wide red stripes around the lower part of the tree trunk. After that, she took off all her fine clothes and tied them to the fork of the tree, as an offering. When she had stepped aside, in an old, ragged dress that she had been wearing under her good one, all the other people came up and tied their offerings of food or clothes to the fork of the tree. Last of all, the Sun Dance chief tied little painted rawhide images of a man and a buffalo to the tree trunk. This was to show that the dance was given to the sun by men, in gratitude for the buffalo. Then all the men joined in carrying the tree back to the camp. There they ceremoniously set the tree in place in the middle of the camp circle.

The next day all the men went out together to cut logs. The men brought the logs back to camp, and placed them around the center pole. The logs were set in a circle about

forty feet across, their lower ends planted in the earth as if they were still growing trees. Each pair of logs was about ten feet apart. The men tied big beams from the center post out to the circle of logs. Then they tied beams from the fork of one upright post to that of the next. All the logs were tied together with rawhide ropes. The ropes bound the whole lodge together, so that it would always stand firm. The men tied their ropes so securely that many years after the last Sun Dance was held, in 1890, the lodge where it had been given was still standing.

On the third of the getting-ready days, all the people of the tribe gathered willow branches to cover the lodge. The green leafy boughs made a shade, so the hot sun would not burn the dancers. Everybody took part in this work: men, and women, and children. The people all wore their finest buckskin clothes, and they rode out into the woods together, singing. This was the one time of the year when a young man and woman who were not married might ride on the same horse. In fact, if a young man asked a girl to ride with him, it was the same as asking her to marry him.

Late in the afternoon of the third day, the people all rode back to camp. They were singing, and they wore wreaths of green willow branches on their heads. The people beat time to their singing with green willow branches which they held in their hands. Behind the horses, and tied to them with ropes, were whole willow trees to be used to cover the lodge. The singing people rode four times around the framework of the lodge.

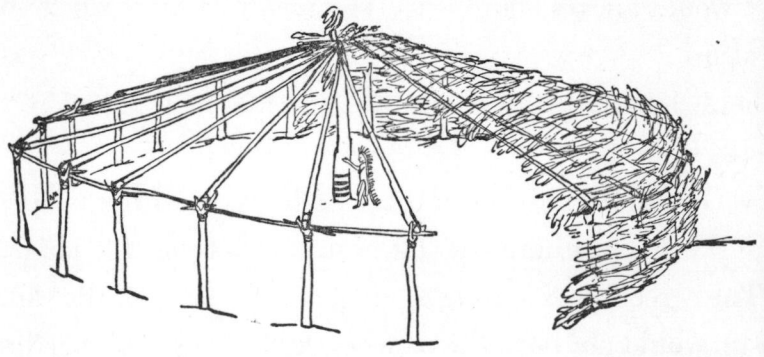

They did not go inside it. Then the men untied the willow boughs their horses had been dragging, and then the men covered the lodge with the leafy branches. When they did this work, the men were always careful to leave an open doorway on the east side of the lodge.

The fourth of the getting-ready days was called "the Day of Opening the Lodge." In some ways it was the most important day of the whole ceremony. Early in the morning, the word went through the camp, "The Mud Heads are coming!" That was the signal for the women to gather up everything that they owned, and to get all the things safely inside the teepees. If anything were left lying around outside, the Mud Heads had the right to pick it up and throw it away, or to break it or spoil it. The Sun Dance chief chose the men who were to act as clowns and nobody else knew who they were. The Mud Heads coated their bodies with mud, and wore mud-coated buckskin masks to hide their faces. Some of the clowns pretended to be horses, and carried other men on their backs like riders. One Mud Head might pretend to be a woman, with a bundle of rags on his back for a baby. The woman would have a pretend-husband running behind her and whipping her with his ridingwhip.

All the people ran inside their teepees when they saw the Mud Heads coming, for fear that they would be whipped, too. After the Mud Heads had gone by, the people came out and watched them, and had fun seeing what the Mud Heads did to each other.

On the same day, after the Mud Head parade, came the big opening parade for the Dance. All the societies took part in this procession. The men all wore their society dance costumes, like wearing uniforms. With the Sun Dance chief leading them, the societies rode slowly through the camp, and then over to the lodge. When the members of the societies were all gathered inside the lodge, a man rode in with the hide of a newly killed year-ling buffalo bull. This man had to go out early in the morning of the Day of Opening the Lodge, and he had to shoot the buffalo with a single arrow, if the dance were to go right. The Sun Dance chief took the hide from the hunter, and tied it with the other offerings, in the fork of the center pole. Then everything was ready for the Sun Dance to begin.

The Sun Dancers were always men. Most of them were young. They danced because they had made prom-ises or vows to do so. Men made the vows because they or their relatives were sick, and they thought that danc-ing in the Sun Dance was a way to recover health. A man also promised to dance in the Sun Dance because he wanted success in hunting or fighting, or because he wanted health throughout a long life to come. Sometimes a woman made a Sun Dance vow, if she or her children were sick, but she didn't dance herself. Her husband or brother danced for her.

The dancers went into the lodge on the evening of the fourth getting-ready day. With each dancer there went an old man. The old man was the dancer's teacher, and showed him what to do during the ceremony. A man took the same place inside the lodge that his teacher had

had when he first danced. The Sun Dance chief sat in a little, leafy shelter on the west side of the lodge. Behind him there was hung a doll-like image that represented the Sun Dance power.

Now, when the men were all inside the lodge and ready, the dance could begin. The dancers took off all their clothes except their breechclouts and moccasins. The teachers painted each of the dancers with blue and yellow and green paint. Everybody was forbidden to wear red clothes or paint during the Sun Dance.

Then the teachers tied green willow branches to the dancers' heads and wrists and ankles. Each teacher gave the dancer he was helping an eagle wingbone whistle, with white feathers from an eagle's breast tied to it. The dancers stood in a curving line, facing the Sun Dance chief and the doll that hung behind him. The teachers sat in their places around the walls of the lodge. When everybody was in line, the teachers began to drum and sing. The dancers stood still, lifting their feet up and down in time with the singing.

All the dances of the four dancing days were the same as the first one. At the end of every fourth song, the Sun Dance chief took a crow wing feather fan, and with it in his hand he chased the dancers four times around the

The Sun Dance

lodge. Then the dancing men could lie down and rest for a while. They were allowed to rest and sleep, but during the four days of dancing the men were not permitted to eat or drink. Their teachers were not allowed to eat or drink, either.

Sometimes, after a man had starved and thirsted for two or three days, he would be so weak that he would fall down when the Sun Dance chief chased him. Then the man's teacher would help him up, and lead him back to his place by the wall of the lodge. Some men said they saw visions of their spirit guardians or of other spirits when they were unconscious at these times. Other men did not claim to have seen visions. But whether a man had a vision or not, if he went through the whole four days of the Sun Dance without eating or drinking, he knew that his vow was fufilled and that his prayers would be answered.

Every night, after the day's dancing ended at sundown, the dancers stayed in the lodge. They were not allowed to leave it until the end of the ceremony. But during the same time there was feasting and celebration in camp. Families held give-aways. Members of other tribes came and visited, and feasts were given for them. The Sun Dance was like our Christmas, a time of good will and happiness for everybody. All the people felt peaceful and contented. No war parties started out, and other tribes did not attack a Sun Dance camp. It was a time for everybody to feel secure.

After the four days of the Sun Dance, when the Sun Dance chief had chased the dancers around the lodge for the last time, and this time had chased them clear outside the shelter, the camp broke up and the families scattered out again. They went away so as to make the most of the good summer grass, while it was still green and fresh, before the heat had browned and dried it. The people could not stay on where they were, because in eight days the horses had eaten all the grass around the camp, and there was no feed left for them.

Before they left the camping place, the Sun Dance chief called all the people together and blessed them. At the same time, he told them where he thought the Sun Dance would be held in the coming year. He told the people this so that they could begin to gather in towards the place when they felt that the time was about right for them to go there. Then the tribe broke up into bands and families, and the smaller groups spread out over the plains to wait for the next year to come.

7

INDIAN DOCTORS AND MEDICINES

WHENEVER PEOPLE get sick, they wonder about the things that caused the sickness, and try to figure out what those things were. This is so they can avoid them in the future, and not get sick in the same way another time. Nowadays we know that most sicknesses are caused by microbes, but there was a time when our great-grandparents thought that bad dreams or night air could make you sick. That was before our doctors had discovered that there were such things as microbes.

Like our own ancestors, the Plains Indians had never heard about microbes or about the diseases that microbes cause. They had never heard about hospitals or scientific laboratories or penicillin or vaccinations. But the Plains Indians did believe in spirits, and they thought and talked about the spirits a great deal. So it was that they came to believe that evil spirits caused diseases.

The bad spirits were supposed to make people sick by shooting them with magic weapons, like stones or cactus thorns, or with little sharp teeth of wild animals. When a person became ill, it was believed that one of the magic weapons had been shot into his body by a spell. The way to make the sick person well, the Indians believed, was to remove the magic weapon.

The Indians did not think that everybody knew how to get it out. To heal sick people, they believed, a man had to be so good himself that all the good spirits were on his side, fighting with him. Then he was strong enough to drive out the evil spirits, and he could be a doctor. We feel a good deal the same way about our doctors, and we expect them to be good men, always.

The Indian doctor, when he was called on to heal somebody, came and sat beside the sick person and asked him many questions, just as our doctors do. He needed to know where the patient's pain was, and if it were a steady pain, or one that came and went. The doctor wanted to know everything that the patient had been doing before he felt sick; where he had been; whom he had seen; and what he had said to people or they had said to him. This was to make sure that the evil spirit had come into the sick person's body from outside, and had not been put there by something wrong that he himself had done or said.

When the doctor had found out everything that he could by asking questions, he went to work to treat the patient. All of the doctors sang songs and rattled gourds, and some of the doctors danced. This was so that the evil spirits would know that the good spirits were coming to fight them, and to encourage the good spirits to fight hard.

When the doctor believed that he had sung and had shaken his rattle long enough, according to the rules that his spirit guardian had given him; he took a small stone knife and cut an "X" on the patient's skin, over the place where the pain was worst. The doctor sucked at the cut as quickly and lightly as he could. After four tries, the doctor would pretend to suck out the magic weapon that had made the patient sick. The doctor would hold the weapon up in his hand, and show it to everybody in the sick person's family. Then the doctor would throw the weapon in the fire, so that the evil spirits couldn't get it back and use it again to hurt somebody else. This was the magical part of the treatment.

Not all of the curing was magical, though. After the Indian doctor had taken out the magic weapon, he would

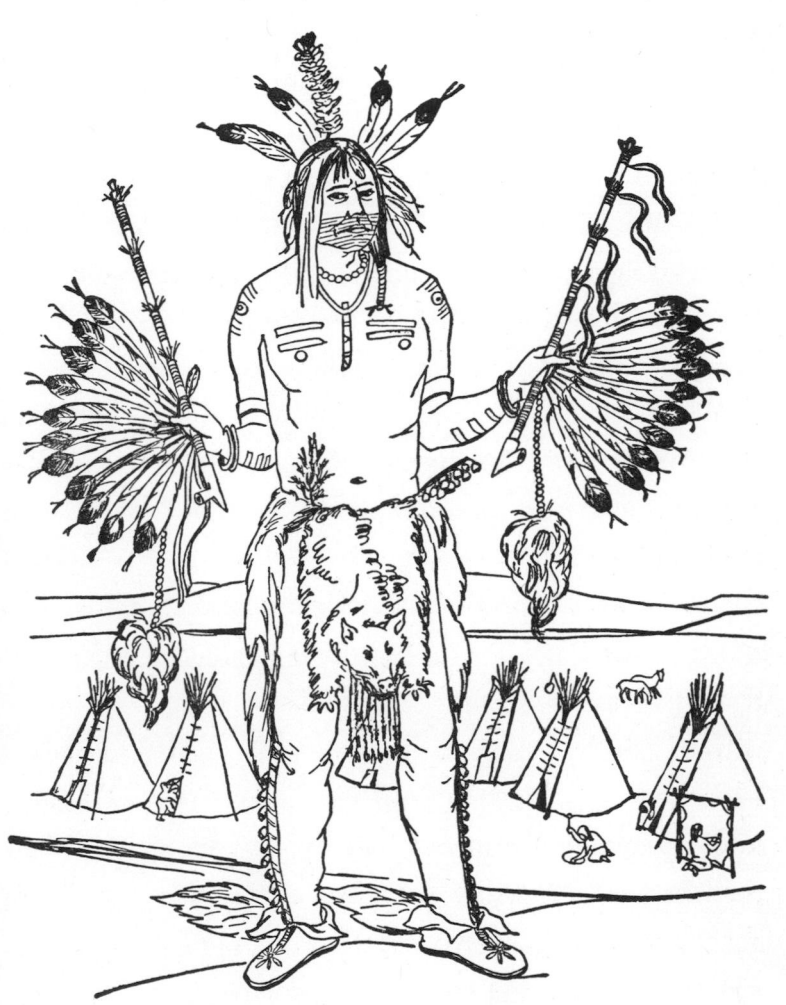

An Indian Doctor

tell his patient to lie quiet and to rest; to eat light food and not too much of it, just as our doctors tell us to do when we are sick. Often the Indian doctor would give the family special instructions about bathing the patient. He would give them herbs to make into teas for the patient to drink. Some of these herbs, such as peyote cactus and wild sage and mint, were so good for certain diseases that we still use them today. The rules were all like those our doctors make for their patients to follow.

The Plains Indians did not believe that people who were hurt in accidents, or men who were injured in fighting, had been hurt by evil spirits. Everybody knew that if a man fell off his horse and broke his leg, he wouldn't be able to walk or ride for a while. Nobody believed that an evil spirit had got into the horse to make the rider fall. It was just an accident that had happened.

When there was an accident, or when a man had been hurt in fighting, there were special doctors in some tribes, who were called on to take care of the person who had been hurt. These men were called Buffalo Doctors. They wore headdresses made out of the scalps of buffalo bulls; and they stamped their feet and roared like buffaloes when they danced. Besides dancing and singing, the Buffalo Doctors did other things to help their patients.

A Healing Ceremony

We call some of the things that they did first aid, and we think that everybody should know about them.

The most important thing that the Buffalo Doctors did was to keep everything near the injury as clean as possible. They washed cuts with hot water, and bandaged them with strips of soft, clean deer hide. Sometimes the Buffalo Doctor would put a dressing of warm, clean fat over a cut, to keep the dirt out of it. If an arm or a leg were broken, the Buffalo Doctor put on splints that were as good as any that we know about today. The splints were made out of stiff, hard pieces of rawhide, and tied in place with strips of soft-tanned skin. The Buffalo Doctors even knew how long to leave the splints on the injuries, so the bones would knit right and the arm or leg would be well again.

Because they lived outdoors and their life was active; and because they ate plain foods and few sweets, the Plains Indians were generally healthy people.

Until the white people came on the plains, in about 1850, the Indians there had never had mumps or measles or smallpox. They had never had colds or pneumonia or tuberculosis. These were all diseases that the white people brought with them from Europe, and that the Indians caught from them. Because the Indians had never had these sicknesses before, their bodies were not able to resist the diseases, and many of the Indians died suddenly in a short time. European diseases still make Indians sicker than they do white people. Getting new sicknesses in this way has been one of the worst things that have happened to the Plains Indians. Their doctors did not know how to treat these new diseases, or get rid of the microbes that caused them.

8

A PLAINS INDIAN COOKBOOK

ΛΛΛΛΛΛΛΛΛΛΛΛΛΛΛΛΛΛΛΛΛΛΛΛΛΛΛΛΛΛΛΛΛ

SINCE THE Plains Indians could not read or write their languages, they never put their knowledge down on paper. Everything that they knew they had to remember from word-of-mouth teaching. Cooking was remembered and taught in the same way that other subjects were.

Because a girl had to know and remember everything about foods, she started learning about them when she was very small. First, she went with her mother and the other women to gather fruits and berries. Later, when she was older, she went with the women who followed the hunters to skin and butcher the game. When the meat had been brought back to the teepee, the girl learned to preserve it for winter use.

By the time that a girl was ready to marry, she had learned to be a good cook, and to take care of everything that she used in preparing food. She learned to keep all her kitchen tools clean and ready to use. If a girl did not know these things, and if she were not careful about doing them, people did not think that she was ready to marry.

Although the Plains Indians ate more meat than any other food, they knew about and used many roots, berries, and other plants that grew in their country. The Indians had no cows or goats, and nobody was ever able to tame the buffalo, so the Indians lacked milk, butter and cheese. They had no chickens, but they ate the eggs of wild birds, when they found nests. In most ways the food that the Plains Indians ate was good, even though it was different from ours.

The most important meat to the Plains Indians was that of the buffalo. There were many different ways of cooking this meat. The easiest way was to put a slice of the meat on a green stick, and hold it or hang it over the fire. Meat cooked like this was half broiled, half roasted, and it tasted very good. When a woman wanted extra seasoning for her meat, she made the broiling fire of pecan or hickory wood. The wood smoke flavored the buffalo meat, just as it does our ham or bacon.

If she had plenty of time, and if the meat were tough, the woman boiled it. The most famous way was by means

of stone-boiling. To cook meat by this method, the woman first dug a hole in the ground with a sharp-pointed stick. She lined the hole with a clean, freshly scraped hide, and weighted the edges of the skin down with big stones. Then the woman filled the hide with water and chunks of meat. Next, the cook built a fire on top of a pile of clean stones. She was careful to select small, round stones, of a kind that would not explode if they got too hot. When the fire had heated the stones red hot, the woman lifted them from the fire on forked green sticks. She dropped the hot stones into the hideful of meat, being careful not to let the food splash over the edges of the hole onto the ground. As the hot stones were put into the stew, the water and meat were heated until they began to boil. It took a long time to cook a meal in this way, because as the stones cooled they had to be taken out of the stew and reheated in the fire. But the Plains Indians liked their meat better when it was cooked in this way than when it was prepared by any other method.

Another famous way of preparing meat was as pemmican. To make this dish, the woman sliced buffalo or deer meat so that it was as thin as paper. Then she hung the meat over racks that she had built of poles, and she set the racks outside her teepee, so the sun could dry and cook the meat. The woman brought her meat indoors at night, so the damp night air would not spoil it. After about four days of sunning, the meat was so dry that it was brittle. It tasted a little like our dried smoked beef. Sometimes meat was stored as soon as it was dried, without any other preparation.

If she wanted to make pemmican, though, the woman took her dried meat and put it in a wooden bowl, or on a stiff, dry hide. Then she pounded and pounded the meat with a stone hammer, until the beef was powdered fine. Next, if the woman had berries or fruits that she had dried, she added them to the pounded meat, and pounded

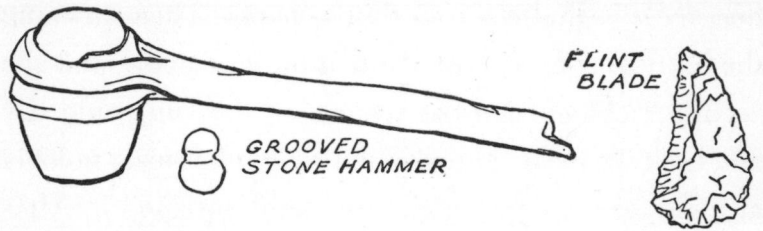

and mixed all the foods together. After that, the woman put the mixture in flat rawhide cases. She sealed the cases by pouring clean melted fat over their openings, and letting the fat harden like paraffin.

Pemmican tasted better than it sounds. In winter, a woman cooked her pemmican just as she did fresh meat, by boiling it with stones. After the Indians got kettles from the white traders, they could cook meat and pemmican in kettles hung over the fires. Pemmican soaked up lots of water, and it took a long time to cook, but when it was done, it made a good stew for cold days. Men on war parties, or children who were playing away from home, carried handfuls of pemmican with them to eat raw. Nobody liked pemmican raw as well as they did when it was cooked, but it was just as nourishing and good for them raw as when it had been made into stew. Pemmican was a sort of Indian K-ration, that could be eaten in any way that was convenient.

When the man of the family had killed a big buffalo, his wife made sausage out of the marrow. She broke up the big leg bones with her hammer, and boiled the pieces of bone to get out all the marrow fat. Then she put the fat into pieces of cleaned intestine, and hung the filled cases up to dry in the sun until she needed the sausage. If she had herbs, like wild sage or wild onions, she added them to the marrow, as seasoning.

Deer meat, or venison, was cooked in the same ways as buffalo beef. So was antelope meat, if a tribe went far enough west to hunt this game. Some Plains Indian tribes ate rabbits, prairie dogs, squirrels, and other small rodents, but most of the Plains Indians did not care for them. The plains peoples very seldom ate fish or waterfowl. They were afraid of things that grew and lived near the water, for large rivers and lakes were not common in the plains country. All of the peoples of the plains ate some game birds, like wild turkeys, quail, and prairie hens. These were all native American birds.

The Plains Indians used salt to season their meat dishes. The salt came from salt beds, where it was on the surface of the ground, or from salt springs, where it was dissolved in the water. When the salt was dry, the Indians dissolved it in water, and then boiled it until the water had evaporated, to be sure it would be clean. A deposit of salt was left on the hide or kettle where the water had been boiled. The woman scraped up the dried salt, pounded it fine, and then put it away in little buckskin bags to use when she needed it. This salt was grayish in color, and rather coarse in texture, but it was better than no salt at all. Water from the salt springs was also boiled, and the salt it had contained was saved in the same way. Sometimes, if a woman had used up all her salt, she might use finely powdered pecan or hickory ashes to season her meat.

Many fruits grew wild on the plains, in summer. There were wild currants and blackberries, wild strawberries and buffalo berries and skunk berries. Later in the season came the wild cherries and the chokecherries; and the sand plums and the tree plums.

The women and girls spent days at a time gathering these fruits and berries. As they picked the fruit, they put it in rawhide bags, since they had no baskets. Late in the fall, the women went out to gather wild grapes from the vines that grew along the creek banks.

The Plains Indians ate some of the wild fruit fresh, as soon as it was gathered. Much of the fruit, though, the women saved for winter. They pounded the fruit first with their stone hammers. Then they made the pounded pulp into cakes which they laid out on clean rawhides to dry in the sun. The cakes of fruit were mixed with dried meat to make pemmican, or were sealed into rawhide cases and stored away, as the pemmican was.

There were wild vegetables, too, to be picked during the spring and summer months. There were lambs' quarters, and poke shoots, and wild spinach. There were wild potatoes, too, and jerusalem artichokes, which grew underground like the potatoes. Some trees and bushes have green sprouts that are good to eat in the spring, and the Indians knew about these and gathered them. A few of the wild vegetables, like potatoes and artichokes which they knew would keep, the women dried and saved as they did fruits.

Because they raised no crops or gardens, the Plains Indians had no grain to make bread. When they were near tribes that grew corn, the Plains Indians traded dried meat or tanned hides for cornmeal, and then they could make mush or hoecakes. Sometimes the Pueblo Indians from New Mexico came east to visit the plains tribes, and they traded the kind of thin cornbread that they call tortillas for hides or meat. After the white people came, the Plains Indians could get flour and meal from them, and then they learned to make bread for themselves.

The tribes who lived in the southwestern part of the plains country also made a meal out of mesquite beans.

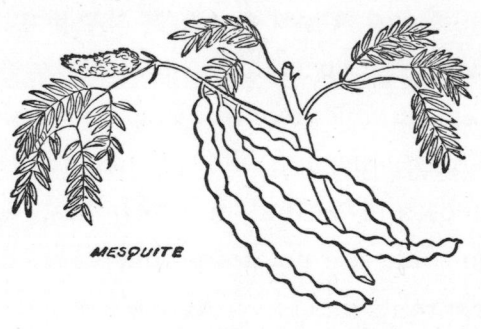

MESQUITE

The beans are very hard when they are dry, and it takes a lot of pounding to crack their shells and get out the kernels. Grinding the beans between two stones is hard work, too. Once the kernels have been ground, they make a fine, light-yellow meal, that looks a little like cornmeal, and seems to have almost no taste. Mesquite meal is one of the strongest foods in the world, though. A pinch of it stirred into a cup of water will give you enough energy to work on all day, if you drink it at breakfast time. Mesquite meal can be eaten dry, too, but, like any other meal, it is choky when it is taken that way. Men who went out on hunting parties or war raids always took mesquite meal with them. As long as they had the meal they could keep traveling without stopping to cook when they got hungry. All they had to do was swallow a little of this food.

For dessert, the Plains Indians ate fresh or dried fruits. When they found a hive of wild bees, the Indians took the honey. In later years, the plains people got sugar and candy from the white traders. The older people didn't like the taste of the sugar or of the things that were made from it, because they were too sweet. So it happened that the little children were the first Indians who learned to eat and like candy.

There were other Plains Indians recipes, besides those that are listed here. These are the most common ones. They are the recipes that every woman knew, to make the dishes that every family liked to eat. All the Plains Indian women were proud of being good cooks and of keeping their families well-fed. In the same way, the men were proud of being good hunters, and of bringing in plenty of game to be cooked for their families.

9

HOW THE PLAINS INDIANS MADE THINGS

ΛΛΛΛΛΛΛΛΛΛΛΛΛΛΛΛΛΛΛΛΛΛΛΛΛΛΛΛΛΛΛ

ALMOST ALL of the things that the Plains Indians made and used began with buffalo or deer hides. This was for two reasons. The first was that since the people were moving around all the time, they did not want to have things that would be heavy to carry with them. The second reason was that the Plains Indians killed many buffalo and deer for food, so they had plenty of hides to use in making things.

There are two main ways of preparing hides for use. The first is by sun-drying, to make rawhide. The second is by rubbing and treating, or tanning, to make soft skin. Each way is important for making special things. The way a skin is to be used determines the way it is prepared.

Making rawhide, of course, was the easier way of treating the skins. When she made rawhide, a Plains Indian woman first fastened the skin she was using flat on the ground. She drove wooden pegs through the edges of the hide and down into the earth. When the skin was spread flat and fastened firmly, the woman took an elbow-shaped tool, with a bone or antler handle and a sharp stone or steel blade, and scraped every bit of meat off the hide. Then the woman turned the hide over, and

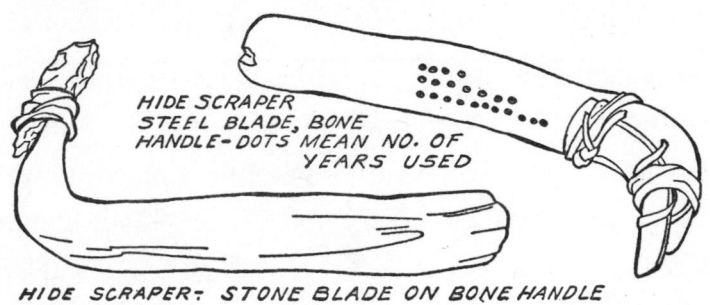

HIDE SCRAPER
STEEL BLADE, BONE
HANDLE-DOTS MEAN NO. OF
YEARS USED

HIDE SCRAPER: STONE BLADE ON BONE HANDLE

again fastened it to the ground. Still using her elbow-shaped tool, she scraped all the hair from the outer surface of the hide. After that, the woman left the hide to dry in the sun for three or four days, and then it was ready to use.

Dry rawhide is nearly as hard as a piece of wood. It is difficult to cut or to work with it in any way. But if rawhide has been made right, it will last a long time, and it is good for making many things that get hard use.

Soft-tanning the hides was slower and harder work

than making rawhide. To soft-tan a hide, the woman stretched it and scraped it as if she were going to make rawhide. After the skin was clean, the woman took the liver and brains of the animal with whose skin she was working, and cooked them with some fat. Then she pounded the meat and fat into a paste. It was a Plains Indian saying that every hide had brains enough to tan itself. After her paste was ready, the woman rubbed it into the flesh side of the hide with a flat stone. It took a lot of rubbing to get all the paste worked into the hide, but the woman had to work without stopping, until the mixture was thoroughly rubbed into the hide. If she stopped too soon, the hide got stiff. Then she had to work it over again, with fresh paste, or use it for rawhide.

When all the paste was rubbed into the skin, the woman sprinkled the hide all over with warm water. She rolled the skin up tightly. Then she put it in a shady place, where it would not get too warm, and left it there for a few days. The skin soaked up every bit of the paste during this time.

Next the woman unrolled the hide. She began rubbing the skin back and forth with her hands, pulling and stretching it, and working with the skin to soften it. This work, too, took her a long time. A woman might have to

Preparing a Hide for Tanning

work for a whole day to get a big skin soft. And while she was doing this part of the work, too, the woman could not stop except for a few minutes at a time, to eat and rest. If she let the skin dry out, even a little, she had to start all over again. When a hide had been soft-tanned in the right way, it was as soft as cloth, and just as easy to cut. The soft skin was a creamy white color. A soft-tanned hide was not waterproof, so if it got wet it would harden and stiffen, and would have to be worked all over again.

Soft-tanned hides could be made waterproof by smoking them. Many different plants were used to make the smoke. Some tribes used cedar or juniper branches or roots. Others used fungus growths from the roots or trunks of trees, while still others used wild grasses or weeds.

The most important thing was to make a fire that gave

SMOKING
A HIDE

FINAL
WORKING
OF HIDE

very little flame and a lot of smoke. When the fire was smouldering, a frame of sticks, like the frame of the teepee, was built over it. Then the hide was stretched and tied over the sticks, and was left to smoke for several hours. The woman watched the hide closely, to be sure that the fire did not go out, or that the skin did not get too dry and start to burn.

After a skin had been smoked, it was hung up outside the teepee to air for a while, before it was used. Smoked hides, even those many years old, usually smell a little of the smoke. The smoked skins are golden-brown in color, and are even softer to touch than are the white soft-tanned skins. When people speak of "buckskin color," they are usually thinking of the color of a smoked hide.

Rawhide was used to make moccasin soles; for the cases that held clothing or dried foods; and for ropes and saddles. These, and other articles that were made of rawhide, were things that got hard use, and had to be made of a material that would wear well.

Soft-tanned hides were used to make the moccasin uppers; and for dresses, shirts, leggings, teepees, and bedding. Hides were soft-tanned to make winter wraps, but the hair was left on them so that they would be extra warm. Smoked hides were often used for making moccasin uppers, or for clothing to be worn in wet weather.

The thread that was used for sewing all of these things was made of sinew from a deer or buffalo. The sinew of the animal that can be used for thread is the large, heavy muscle that lies along either side of the backbone. These muscles can be cut out of the meat in long, flat strips. After the meat scraps have been scraped away and the sinews have been dried, the muscle fibres can be separated from one another into long, fine threads. If the sinew thread is moistened a little when it is used, the natural glue that is found in all animal fibers will cause the threads to stick to each other, and to the skins that are being sewn together. This makes sinew thread the best to use in sewing moccasins or clothes that are made of leather.

Because they had no needles, the Plains Indian women made awls, or thrusting points, to sew with. At first the women used finely pointed pieces of bone or stone, but after the white traders brought them metal, in about 1850, the women had steel awls. In sewing with an awl, a woman made holes in the skin, one at a time, and then threaded the sinew through the holes. This was a slower way of sewing than with a needle, but the sinew could be pulled tight and the work made very firm.

In most of the Plains tribes, both the men and the women were saddle makers. The saddle frames were made of forked tree limbs, or of buffalo rib bones, or of elk antlers. The pieces of the frame were tied together with wet rawhide ropes. Rawhide, when it is wet, will stick to things just the same way that sinew does, so the process was like tying and gluing the pieces at the same time.

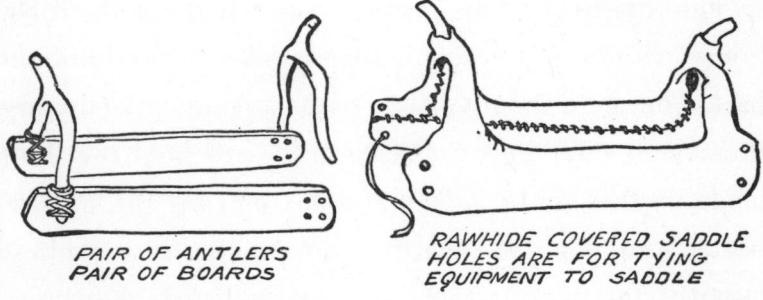

PAIR OF ANTLERS
PAIR OF BOARDS

RAWHIDE COVERED SADDLE
HOLES ARE FOR TYING
EQUIPMENT TO SADDLE

After the ropes that held the frame together were thoroughly dry, the saddle cover was put over the frame. This was done by soaking a large piece of rawhide in water, and then cutting it into the right shape. Then the cover was sewn over the frame with wet rawhide strings. When the cover had dried and set, the saddle was as solid as if it had a metal frame.

The halters that went on the horses' heads were made of rawhide ropes or of braided strips of soft-tanned hide.

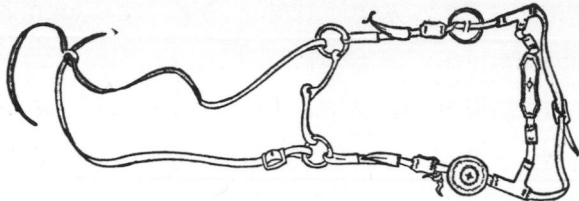

A Cheyenne Silver Bridle

Sometimes the halters were trimmed with metal ornaments or with beadwork.

The Plains Indians usually rode without stirrups. Some men did not even tie their saddles to their horses' backs, but held them in place by balancing and gripping them with their knees. Pack saddles, to hold the drag loads or the light loads that were tied on the horses' backs, were made in the same way as the riding saddles. Usually, the pack saddles were made with higher pommels and horns than were the riding saddles.

The rawhide cases which the Plains Indians used to hold their food and clothing were shaped rather like envelopes. To make a case, a hide was laid out flat on the ground. The shape of the case was marked out with a knife point, and then the hide was cut into shape. The places where the folds of the envelope were to be were pressed down with the blunt edge of the knife, so the hide would bend easily along the lines. Holes were cut in the ends of the envelope flaps, and soft hide strings were passed through the holes.

When one of these cases was to be packed, it was laid out flat. Then the articles it would hold were laid out on top of the case. Then the side flaps were turned up over the contents and were tied together. Last of all, the end flaps were tied on the outside of the case. An envelope made and packed like this would hold many things, but still it was flat and easy to carry. The cases are often called "parfleches," which is a French name for anything made of rawhide.

Rawhide ropes were used for a great many purposes. Usually, when a woman wanted to make a rope, she first soaked the rawhide in water, to make it pliable and easy to work. Then the skin was cut into one long strip with a knife. To cut the hide, the woman began at the outer edge and went around and round the skin, pulling the strip of hide out straight and flat as she cut it. If the cutting were done in the right way, a whole skin made one flat, even string. This big cord could then be divided into shorter lengths, to be used as they were needed.

Usually four strips of rawhide were braided together to make a rope. If the rope were to be extra strong, six or eight strips of skin were used. If only a light cord were needed, two pieces of rawhide were twisted together by rolling them between the palms of the woman's hand, or over her knee. All the time that the hide was being braided or twisted, the woman kept it wet. Afterwards, she coiled the rope, and let it dry out very slowly, so it would not get hard or brittle. Last of all she rubbed the rope with fat to keep it pliable. Some ropes made by Plains Indian workers have lasted as long as a hundred years, and they are still strong and supple enough to use today.

Both rawhide and soft-tanned skins were used in making a pair of moccasins. Moccasin making was the work that the Indian women had to do most often. Moccasins are light shoes, so they wear out quickly. A Plains Indian woman always had her sewing bag with her. In it she had moccasins cut out and ready to make up for the different members of her family.

To make a pair of moccasins, the woman first asked the person who was going to wear them to stand flat on a piece of rawhide. Then the woman took a stick of charcoal from the fire, and drew the outlines of the wearer's feet on the hide. After she had done this, she cut the footprints out of the hide with her knife, and the moccasin soles were ready to be used.

Next, the woman took a piece of soft-tanned hide, and

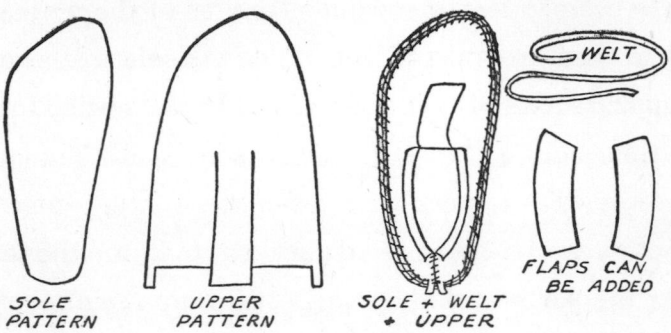

SOLE
PATTERN

UPPER
PATTERN

SOLE + WELT
+ UPPER

WELT

FLAPS CAN
BE ADDED

cut out the upper parts of the moccasins, measuring them against the soles to be sure that they would fit smoothly. Then she cut a narrow strip of soft hide, to sew between the sole and upper of each moccasin. A strip like this is called a welt, and it acts as a pad for the sole of the moccasin, and makes the shoe wear better. Welts are used in fitting our shoe soles today.

When the woman had all the different parts of the moccasins cut out, she was ready to begin sewing. She punched holes through the upper, the welt, and the sole with her awl, and then put her sinew thread through the holes. The woman used an over-and-over sewing stitch, like the stitch that we use in making a hem in a dress or skirt. The woman was always careful not to tie knots in her sinew thread, because the knots might rub the wearer's feet, and make sore places.

The woman began sewing at the toe of the moccasin, and worked around the outside of the sole to the heel. Then she broke off her thread, and began sewing again, this time making the seam along the instep of the foot. In this way the uppers and soles were fitted together smoothly, and there were no puckered places in the seam. After the parts of the moccasin had been sewn together on the wrong side, the moccasin was turned right side out, so that the seam would not show. If all the work had been done just right, a moccasin fitted smoothly, and was firm, but not tight. About eight pairs of moccasins could be made from one deerskin.

All the clothing of the Plains Indians was also made from soft-tanned skins. Men wore moccasins, shirts, high leggings, breechclouts, and belts. Women wore dresses, leggings, and belts. The children dressed like the grown-ups. Nobody wore any regular underclothes, but in cold weather the Indians sometimes put on two or three shirts or dresses at once, in order to keep warm.

The men's leggings and breechclouts together took the place of trousers. A breechclout was just a long strip of soft hide, drawn between the man's legs, and fastened under his belt. Strips or flaps of the skin were left hanging over the belt in front and back, like narrow aprons.

A man's leggings were also fastened to his belt. They were tied at the sides with strips of hide. The leggings were fitted close to the man's legs. If the leggings had been loose, they would have caught on things and been in the way when the man walked or rode. If the leggings were made to be worn for ceremonies, or other times when the man wanted to dress up, they had long fringes down the side seams on the outsides of the legs. It usually took a whole deer hide to make each leg of a pair of plain leggings. Another whole hide was needed to make the fringes on the decorated leggings.

It took at least four deer hides to make a man's shirt. One skin was used for the front and one for the back. Each sleeve was made out of a separate skin. The men's shirts fitted loosely, and were worn outside the belts, like sport shirts.

The women's leggings were shorter than the men's. They came up only to the wearer's knees, so one hide would usually make a pair of woman's leggings. These leggings were not made with fringes, since the women's dresses were long and the leggings did not show much.

It took six deer hides to make a woman's dress. There were two skins in the skirt; two in the blouse; and two in the sleeves. Sometimes the skirt and blouse were sewn or

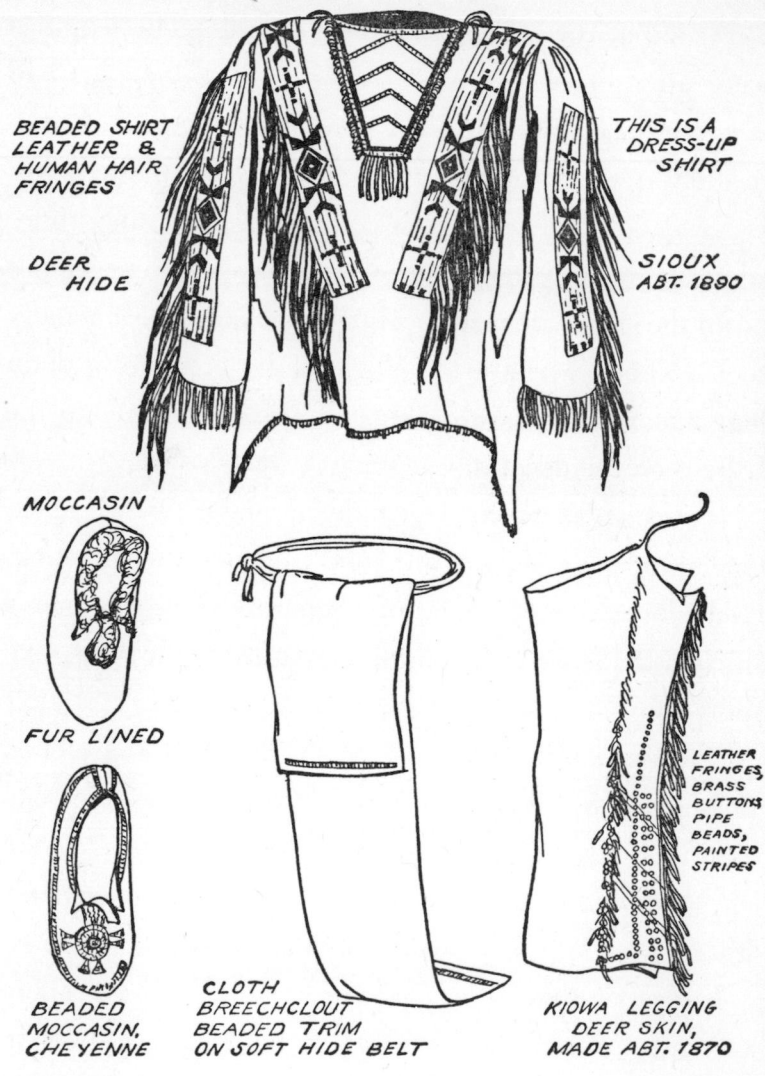

BEADED SHIRT
LEATHER &
HUMAN HAIR
FRINGES

DEER
HIDE

THIS IS A
DRESS-UP
SHIRT

SIOUX
ABT. 1890

MOCCASIN

FUR LINED

BEADED
MOCCASIN,
CHEYENNE

CLOTH
BREECHCLOUT
BEADED TRIM
ON SOFT HIDE BELT

LEATHER
FRINGES,
BRASS
BUTTONS,
PIPE
BEADS,
PAINTED
STRIPES

KIOWA LEGGING
DEER SKIN,
MADE ABT. 1870

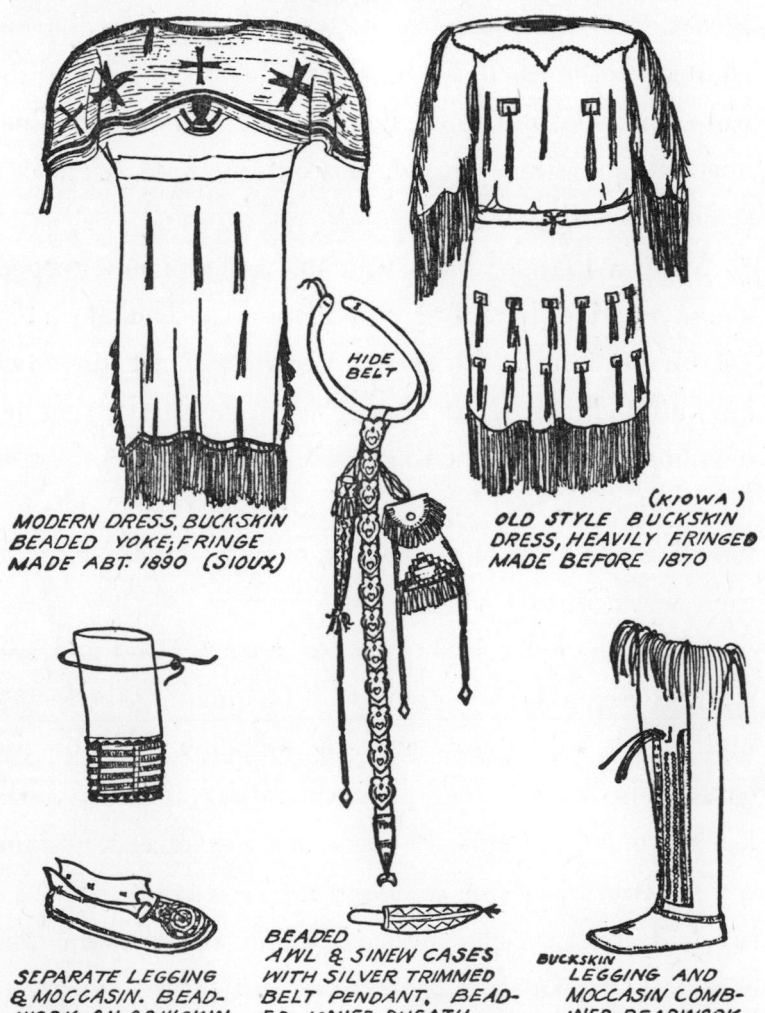

MODERN DRESS, BUCKSKIN
BEADED YOKE; FRINGE
MADE ABT. 1890 (SIOUX)

HIDE BELT

(KIOWA)
OLD STYLE BUCKSKIN
DRESS, HEAVILY FRINGED
MADE BEFORE 1870

SEPARATE LEGGING
& MOCCASIN. BEAD-
WORK ON COWSKIN.
(CHEYENNE)

BEADED
AWL & SINEW CASES
WITH SILVER TRIMMED
BELT PENDANT. BEAD-
ED KNIFE SHEATH
← KIOWA →

BUCKSKIN
LEGGING AND
MOCCASIN COMB-
INED. BEADWORK,
BRASS BUTTONS.

tied together, but sometimes the dress was made in two pieces. A woman wore her belt outside her dress. On the right side of her belt, where she could reach it easily, she wore her knife, and on the left side were her sewing tools; her awl, and sinew thread, and cut-out work, each in a separate small case.

When a Plains Indian woman needed a new teepee, she saved hides for a long time to make it. To make a teepee for her family, the woman needed at least thirty-two big buffalo hides. If the woman were in a hurry to get her new home finished, she might ask her neighbors to trade her some hides that they had tanned. Then she gave her friends meat, or small deer skins, or helped them out with their work, in exchange.

After all of her buffalo hides were soft-tanned and ready to be sewn, the woman who was making the teepee invited her friends to come and help her work on the cover. The women made a sewing party of this work. Every woman brought her own sewing materials, and the woman who was going to live in the new teepee cooked a big feast for everybody. Usually one woman, who was especially good at doing such work, cut out the hides that were to be used for the teepee cover. The cutter gave each of the other women a share of the sewing, and told each worker how to fit the pieces together. All the women sat in a group, and sewed and talked, and at the end of the day the teepee cover was finished.

The poles for the teepees were cut in the high mountains on the western edge of the plains. The poles were usually made of cedar wood, because that wood dried evenly and lasted for a long time. The teepee poles were about twenty feet tall, and about twelve inches around. All of the branches and bark were stripped off the trunk of the tree, and the wood was trimmed down until the whole pole was of an almost even thickness. The upper ends of the poles were tapered a little, so that they could be gathered together and tied in a bunch. Some tribes used twenty poles for the frame works of their teepees, some twenty-two, and some twenty-four.

When a woman wanted to set up her teepee, she tied three or four of the poles together, a few feet from the top. She set the poles on the ground in a triangle if there were three; or in a square if there were four of them. She spread the lower ends of the base poles wide apart, so there would be plenty of room inside the teepee. Then she leaned her other poles against the first ones, filling in the spaces between the base poles. Last of all, the woman tied the secondary poles to the base poles by winding her rawhide rope tightly around the whole bunch. After the poles were bound together, the end of the rope was left hanging down beside the teepee door. Then the poles could be separated quickly, by taking hold of the rope and unwinding it. The door was an open space that was left between two of the poles on the east side of the teepee.

After all the poles were set up, the hide teepee cover was put over them. Two small poles were used to raise the cover into place. They were left tied to the cover, and hung down beside the door, to be used in regulating the opening at the top of the teepee, where the smoke from the fire went out. The fire was lighted in a hole in the middle of the teepee floor. The smoke flaps, or teepee ears, could be moved about when the wind changed its direction, so that the top of the teepee acted as its own chimney. The Plains Indians never built big fires inside their teepees. In fact, they had a saying that meant, "White man builds a big fire, stands a long way off, and freezes to death. Indian builds a little fire, stands close to it, and keeps warm."

The Indians had their own fire-making tools when they first went onto the Plains. All of the early fire tools

they had were made of wood. To light a fire in those days, an Indian man first laid a piece of hard wood, like hickory, pecan, or bois d'arc, flat on the ground. Then he set an upright stick of the same hard wood on the flat board. He took a small bow, with a sinew cord string, and fastened the bow string loosely around the upright stick. Then the man pulled the ends of the bow back and forth, making the upright stick revolve against the flat one.

The friction of the rubbing finally heated the board

until it began to smoke and glow. At the first sign of smoke, the man put finely powdered cedar or cottonwood bark against the end of the sharp stick, so the bark would catch fire from the heat of the friction. After the bark, too, was glowing, the man dumped it on small shavings, or dry leaves, or bigger pieces of bark, so that these things would catch fire. The last stage of fire-making by friction was to take the little fire that had been started, and put it against the wood of the main cooking fire. Making fire in this way was slow work, and it was tiring for the man who did it.

Later, after about 1850, when the white traders and soldiers brought them pieces of metal, the Plains Indians learned to strike the metal against pieces of stone, so that sparks would pop out. This is the same way that cigarette lighters work. Instead of catching the sparks on cotton wicks, though, the Indians caught them on bark or leaves. After the first sparks caught, the fire was lighted as if it had been started by rubbing. Still later, about 1880, when the white people began bringing them, the Indians were able to get matches, and to use them to make fires.

There was very little furniture inside a Plains Indian teepee. There were no chairs or tables; no stools or lamps or small pieces of furniture. The only pieces of furniture that the Plains Indians had were their beds. During the day time, most Indians used their beds as sofas, and sat on them. The beds were set up against the teepee wall, so that the center of the floor, around the fire, could be kept clear.

A Plains Indian bed was set up by putting four forked poles in the ground for the corner posts. Then four other poles were laid across the forks of the uprights, to make a frame. An extra pole was pounded into the ground outside the framework at the head of the bed, and another one at the foot. Slatted mats made of willow rods stitched together with sinew, were fastened to these extra poles. The mats were painted with horizontal stripes of bright colors, and sometimes were ornamented with deerskin tassels. The mats covered the bed frame, and served as springs for the bed.

Hides, tanned with the hair on, were laid over the bed

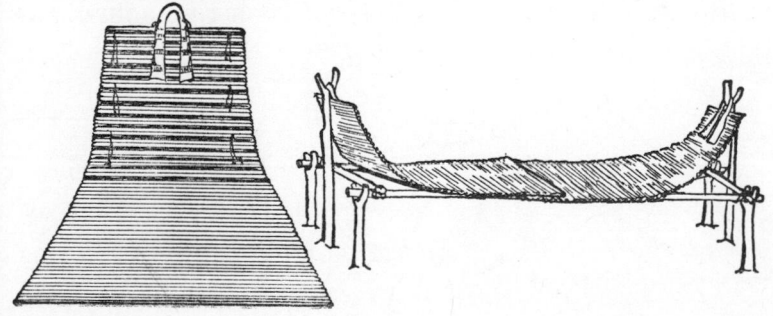

mats. The skins were soft and springy, and they made a warm, comfortable bed. The sheets on these beds were clean, soft-tanned deerskins. All the bedding used by a Plains Indian family was cleaned and aired and shaken daily.

When the family moved camp, the woman of the household took the beds to pieces and tied the poles of each bed together in a bundle. Then she rolled the mats around the poles, and wrapped the bedding around the mats. In this way she made a light, compact bundle of each bed. One horse could carry five or six rolls tied on a pack saddle.

The Plains Indian men made bowls and ladles to be used for cooking and eating. Sometimes the bowls were made of gourds, and the ladles almost always were. Sometimes the bowls were made of burls, or knots, that grew on the roots and trunks of trees. When a man wanted to make a gourd ladle, he took a ripe gourd, and

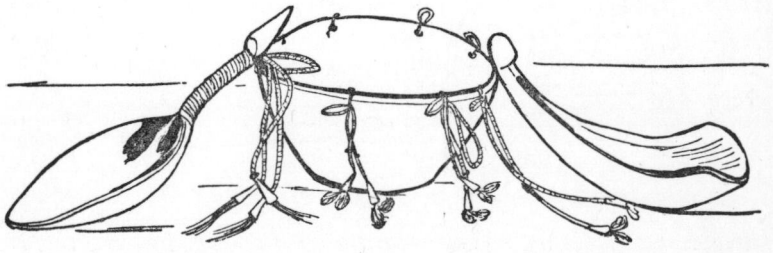

cut it down on one side, so it would be the right size and shape. Then he scraped out the seeds that grew inside the gourd, washed and dried it, and the ladle or bowl was ready to use.

Making a wooden bowl was harder. The man cut a burl from a tree in winter, when the sap was out of the wood. The Plains Indians liked elm or cottonwood burls best, but sometimes they used oak burls. After the man had cut a burl, he hollowed it out by putting live coals on the wood, and letting them burn into it. When the bowl was deep enough, the worker scraped out the charred wood, and shaped the whole inside of the bowl with his knife. After that, he rubbed the inside of the bowl with fine sand, to make it smooth and clean.

Wooden ladles were made in about the same way as the wooden bowls. The men used the small burls that grew on the branches of the tree to make the ladles. They left part of the branch on the burl, to be used as a handle. After a wooden bowl or a ladle had been used for a while, it became smooth and polished, just from handling. Many old bowls, which are kept in our museums, are very beautiful.

Stone hammers were important tools in a Plains Indian household. The women used the hammers to pound up meat and fruit, and to drive teepee stakes into the ground. The men used the hammers when they staked out their horses; or when they pounded bark to use in starting fires; or for weapons in fighting. The men were the ones who made all the hammers.

To make a hammer, a man looked for a stone that was already smooth and rounded from time and wear. The best place to find this kind of stone was in the bed of a creek or river. After the man had found the right sort of stone, he made a groove around it, in the middle. He did this by pulling a wet rawhide string, dipped in sand, back and forth, back and forth, across the stone. The grooving took a long time. When the groove was finished, the stone was ready to be used as a hammer head.

For the handle of the hammer, the man used a piece of hard wood, like bois d'arc or hackberry, with a natural fork in it. The man fitted the grooved stone into the fork of the stick, and tied it there with a wet rawhide cord. As the rawhide dried, it tightened the two pieces of the hammer together. Sometimes a man made a rawhide cover that fitted over the whole hammer, including the handle.

In the days before the white people came to the plains, the Indians there made all their knives, and the points of their spears and arrows, of stone. The men had to hunt for just the right kinds of stone for these tools, too.

Flint was a good kind of stone for making knives and points, and many times the Plains Indians used it. Some white people today call all Indian points "flint arrowheads," because it is an easy name to remember. But just as often as they used flint, the Indians made points out of quartz or jasper. Sometimes they used semiprecious stones like agate or opal. In the northern plains, where there are large beds of volcanic glass, or obsidian, the Indians used that kind of stone. It all depended on where the worker lived, and what kind of stone he could find easily.

When he made a stone point or blade, an Indian man held the rough piece of stone flat against the palm of his left hand. He wore a strip of rawhide tied around the palm of each hand, as a protection. His tool was a piece of deer antler, held in his right hand. The man pressed the antler point down against the stone, with his whole weight. The weight, or pressure, of his right hand against the stone would break off small flakes of stone, one at a time, so this kind of work is called "pressure flaking." Sometimes a piece of stone did not break in the way that the worker expected it to, and had to be thrown away.

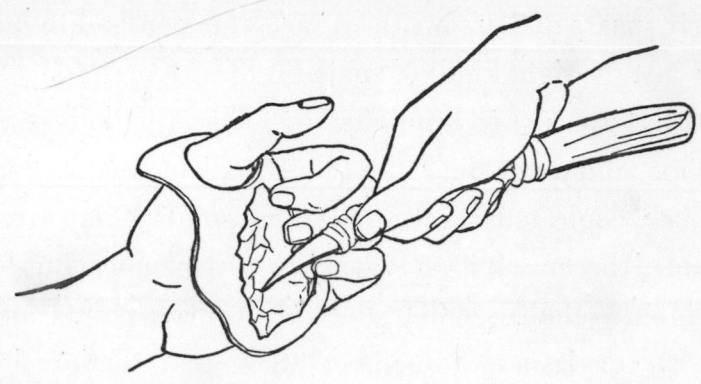

Then the man started over again with another piece of stone.

The Indians never made points by heating the stones and dropping water on them. They knew that most stones, if they are treated in this way, will explode. Then the pieces of stone fly out in all directions, and can cut or even blind someone who is near by.

After the Plains Indian man had made a point, he was ready to fit it to an arrow or a spear. The arrow points had

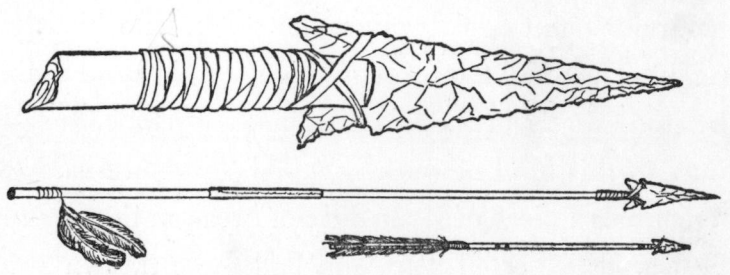

to be made exactly right, so they would balance in the air when they were shot. Spear points did not have to be made so carefully, because the man used his spear for thrusting, and not so much for throwing.

A spear handle was usually made of a round limb from a bois d'arc, hickory, or hackberry tree. The limb was shaped with a stone knife and then was smoothed with fine sand. When the handle was finished, it was about three inches around and four feet long. Then it was ready for the point to be attached.

The man who was making the spear split one end of the handle in two, very carefully, and fitted his stone point into the cut. Then he tied the wood tightly around the point with wet sinew cord. If he wanted them, the man sewed rawhide grips around the spear handle with sinew thread, and the spear was finished. Sometimes the men decorated the handles of their spears with paint and feathers, but often they left the handles plain.

The men used the same woods in making arrow shafts that they used for spear handles. The shafts were shaped and smoothed in the same way that the handles were, but the workers were usually just a little more particular, so the arrows would balance and fly well. Usually the Plains Indian hunters used arrow shafts that were twenty-four to thirty inches long, so the weapons would be easy to use on horseback. Most white men, who shoot on foot, have longer arrow shafts.

The hardest part of making an arrow was the feathering, or fletching. The Plains Indians preferred to use the wing feathers of hawks or eagles for this, but some men used crow or owl feathers. The main thing was to have a feather that was long and straight and strong, and could be fitted to the arrow shaft.

In most of the plains tribes, the old men, who had plenty of time and patience for doing such particular work, were the arrow makers. Since they were often too old to do much hunting themselves, they traded their fine arrows to the other men for meat and hides.

When a man made an arrow, and had the shaft shaped just the way he wanted it, he fitted the feathers on. First he split a feather in half the long way, so its quill, or backbone, could be laid flat against the arrow shaft. He made three vanes, or split feathers, for each shaft. Then he tied the vanes to the shaft with wet sinew string, binding it tightly around the ends of the quills, but leaving the center part, where the feathers branched out, unbound. The combination of tying and gluing, when the sinew dried, was enough to hold the whole quill tightly.

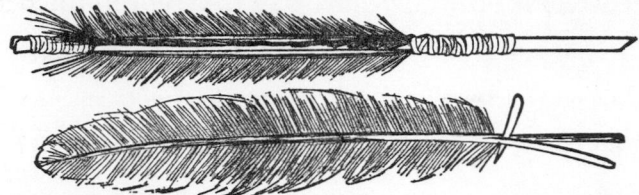

Last of all, the point of the arrow was bound into a cut in the end of the shaft, just as the spear points were tied in. Then the arrow was ready for painting. Every man painted his arrows in his own way. Then, by looking at the painted designs, the men could tell who had shot which animal in the big hunts.

Like the spear and arrows, bows had to be made of hard woods. The Plains Indians preferred bois d'arc, whose French name means "wood of the bow," but they sometimes made their bows out of hickory or hackberry wood. Most Plains Indian men carried three or four lengths of bois d'arc with them at all times, so the wood could season well before it was used. Freshly cut bois d'arc is light lemon yellow in color, but it darkens as it seasons, and an old piece is almost the color of mahogany. If a bois d'arc bow had been carefully made from a piece of well-seasoned wood, it would last a man all his life. Some bows that are over a hundred years old can still be used.

The wood for the bow stave had to be cut in the winter, when the sap was down in the roots of the tree. The best wood was that between the heart of the trunk and the bark, where the wood was hardest and had the fewest knots. After the wood had been thoroughly seasoned, it was worked down smooth and narrow, with a stone knife.

The Plains Indians used bow staves that were about four feet long. This is shorter than the staves that white men use, because a long bow is hard to handle when a man is on horseback. The bow staves were slightly curved, so that the ends flared out and the middle drew in. The ends of the bows were notched to hold the bow cords. The curve in the middle of the stave made a grip for the archer's hand and a brace for the arrow. Sometimes the curve was bound with rawhide, to give the archer a better grip.

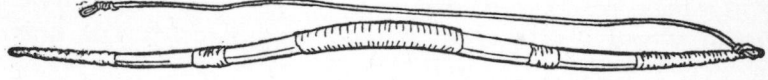

A Plains Indian man was always very careful of his bow. He always loosened the bowstring before he put the bow away, so the stave would not be pulled out of shape or lose its spring. He kept the bow stave, with three or four extra braided sinew cords for strings, in a watertight

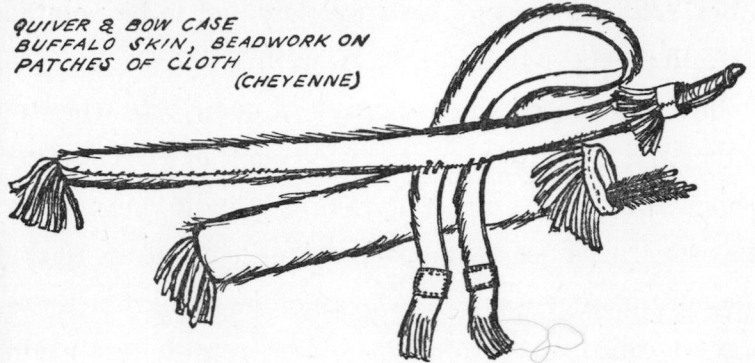

QUIVER & BOW CASE
BUFFALO SKIN, BEADWORK ON
PATCHES OF CLOTH
(CHEYENNE)

rawhide case. He kept his arrows in another, shorter case, which was also waterproof.

In the Plains tribes, pipes were made and used only by the men. Most people know that the Indians invented smoking, and that white people did not know about tobacco until after America was discovered. Often people speak of "Indian peace pipes," as if those were the only pipes the Indians had. They do not stop to think that peace pipes were used in ceremonies, and that there were different kinds of Indian pipes for everyday use.

The kind of pipe that the Plains Indian men used most often was just a straight tube, like a cigarette holder. Often the tubes were made of hollow pieces of bone, usually of deer leg bones. When a man smoked this kind of pipe, he stuffed his tobacco into the end of the tube, and lighted it. Sometimes museum people call these pipes "cloud blowers," because they had to be pointed straight up at the clouds, to draw well.

In the evenings, when a group of men was sitting together and talking, they often used another kind of pipe. This was the stone pipe that people usually mean when they speak of a peace pipe. Instead of being straight, the stem of this pipe was bent like an elbow; and sometimes now we call them "elbow pipes." An extra long wooden stem was added to the stone stem of the pipe, to cool the smoke. The wooden stems were often very beautifully decorated with paint, quills, or beadwork. Not every man owned one of these fine pipes, so it was the custom for each man in the group to take a turn smoking the pipe.

The Plains Indians used a special kind of stone for making their pipes. This stone, which is dull red mottled with white spots, is called catlinite, after the first

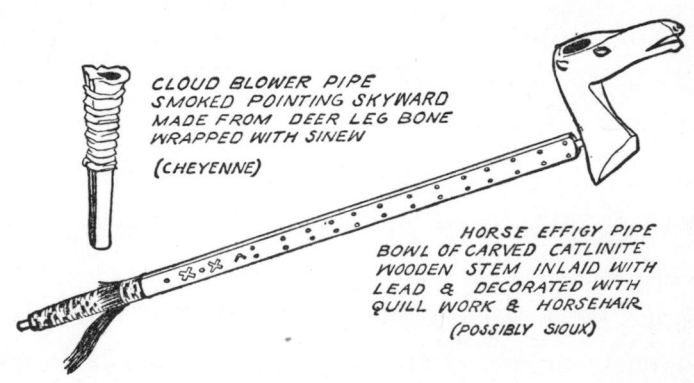

CLOUD BLOWER PIPE
SMOKED POINTING SKYWARD
MADE FROM DEER LEG BONE
WRAPPED WITH SINEW

(CHEYENNE)

HORSE EFFIGY PIPE
BOWL OF CARVED CATLINITE
WOODEN STEM INLAID WITH
LEAD & DECORATED WITH
QUILL WORK & HORSEHAIR
(POSSIBLY SIOUX)

white man to describe it. The stone is found in only one place in the world: a quarry in North Dakota.

When catlinite is first dug up out of the earth, it is very soft and can be cut and shaped like clay. The stone hardens as it dries. After catlinite has been out in the air for a few days, it hardens and has to be worked like sandstone or limestone. The Indians who lived near the catlinite quarry made a practise of digging out the stone, which they called pipestone, and of trading it to other tribes. Because the Indians in the northern plains lived near the catlinite quarry, they had many stone pipes. The tribes in the southern plains, who were farther away, had very few of them.

Because the stone was not easy to get, stone pipes were treasured in most of the Plains tribes. They were used on special occasions, and were handed down from father to son.

In some tribes there were even stone pipes that were believed to be magical. Most of these belonged to the Indian doctors. Other magical pipes belonged to peace chiefs, or to Sun Dance chiefs, and were used in ceremonies.

Since the Plains Indians considered it an honor to be allowed to smoke a stone pipe, the custom arose among them of smoking one when a treaty was signed, or any kind of solemn agreement was made. It was like our custom of kissing the Bible, when a man takes office, or swears that he is telling the truth about something important. This is the custom that people mean when they talk about the Indians smoking a peace pipe. However, the Indians sometimes smoked the same pipes when they made peace and at other times.

In the very earliest days, right after the Plains Indians got their horses, most of the things that the Indians made were undecorated. But as the people traveled about the country, they found beds, or deposits, of brightly colored earths in the new places they visited. Someone had the idea of using the earths as paints, and so the Indians discovered the use of colors.

The earth colors were soft and pale, and we would think that many of them were dull. To people who had no other colors, though, the earths must have appeared brighter and gayer than they do to us. The earth colors that the Plains Indians used were mostly browns, yellows, and reds. Later on, the Indians learned to use berry juices or grape juice for blues, and to mix the juices with yellow earths, to make greens.

After an Indian man had dug up some of the colored

earths, he pounded them with his stone hammer until they were finely powdered. Then he sifted the powder through his fingers, and took out any coarse pieces that had been left in it. He tied each color in a separate buckskin bag, so it would not get mixed up with his other paints. He used the colors for painting anything he wanted to decorate; his weapons, or clothes, or even his face.

When a Plains Indian artist wanted to paint a design on a buffalo hide, he mixed his earth paints with water, putting each color in a small wooden bowl. Then he put a piece of sinew into the bowl with the paint, and left it there for the water to soften. This was like adding glue to his paint. It made the colors stick to the surface of the hide. They would not rub off on his fingers or clothes, if they were stuck down with glue.

The artist used a piece of porous buffalo rib bone as a brush. He put one end of the bone into his paint mixture, and sucked on the other end until the paint had been drawn up into the bone. Then he rubbed the bone over the part of the hide that he wanted to paint. Naturally, he had to have a separate brush for each color he used.

Before he started painting, the Plains Indian artist outlined his design. For this part of the work he used a small piece of bone, pointed like a pencil. He dipped the point of the bone in water, and then pressed it down on the surface of the hide. This made a fine groove in the skin, without leaving any colored line on it. If the artist decided he wanted a colored outline to show, he added it after the rest of the design had been painted in.

There was one thing that was especially interesting about the designs that the Plains Indians used. The men drew pictures of people, animals, and plants. They used these lifelike pictures in decorating the things that they themselves owned and used.

The Plains Indian women, on the other hand, used what our artists call "abstract" designs; that is, figures that are not meant to look like or to suggest the forms of living things. Usually, the designs that the Plains Indian women used were squares, triangles, straight or curved lines, or combinations of these geometric figures.

In time, each artist and each tribe came to like certain designs better than others, and to draw them especially well. This is what our artists call "developing a style." The style development in the plains went on for so long, and grew to be so strong, that people who have studied Plains Indian art can tell, by looking at it, by what tribe a certain piece of painting was made. Sometimes these

Painting a Hide

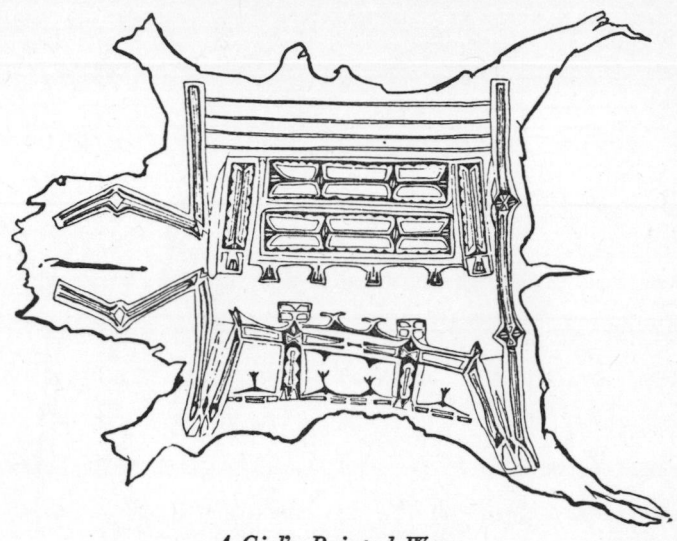

A Girl's Painted Wrap

people can even tell what artist did a certain painting.

In the northern part of the plains, many of the Indian tribes used porcupine quills to trim their clothes, bags, pipe stems, and horse equipment. The Dakota, or Sioux, tribes were especially skillful in this art.

Porcupines are slow, rather stupid, animals. The Indians did not have to chase the porcupines, or even to hunt much to find them, for porcupines live in trees and eat the bark from the branches. So when a Plains Indian woman needed a porcupine for quills, she sent her husband out to get one from the nearest grove of trees.

When the man found the porcupine, he killed it by

hitting it on the head, so the skin was not broken or the
quills damaged. Then he took the porcupine home to his
wife. She pulled the quills out of the porcupine skin very
carefully, one at a time. The quills were loose, and would
come out easily. As she pulled the quills, the woman
sorted them. She put each size in a different buckskin
bag.

Before she used the quills, the woman soaked them in
warm water. Then she took each quill and pulled it flat
between her front teeth, so it looked like a small ribbon.
Then the woman cut off the hard, sharp, outer tip of the
quill, and the quill was ready to sew onto whatever she
wanted to decorate. The quills were stitched in place with
sinew thread.

If the woman wanted to use her quills to trim a rounded
surface, like a pipestem, or the grip of a bow or spear, she
could braid them together into long cords. Then she
wrapped the cords around the surfaces of the things she
wanted to make beautiful. If the braiding and wrapping
were done right, the woman could make a design with the
quills.

Porcupine quills could be colored by boiling them with
earth paints or berries. This took a long time, especially
if the quills had to be boiled with hot stones. Many

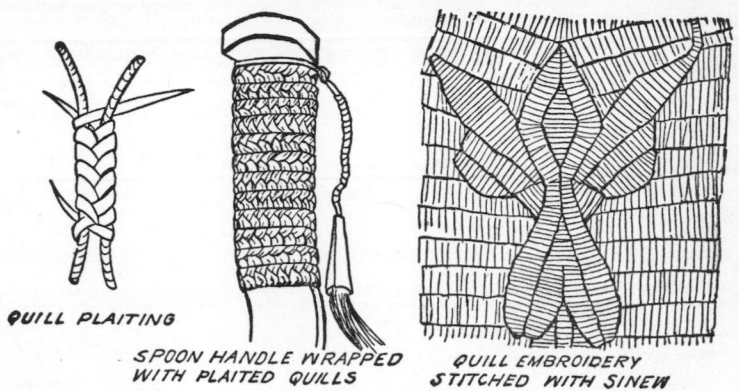

QUILL PLAITING

SPOON HANDLE WRAPPED
WITH PLAITED QUILLS

QUILL EMBROIDERY
STITCHED WITH SINEW

workers liked the natural black and white stripes of the undyed quills, and did not try to change their colors.

After the white traders came onto the plains in the 1850's, they brought the Indians colored glass beads that had been made overseas, in France and Italy and Czechoslovakia. The Indians had never seen or heard of glass beads before that time, and they were delighted with the new way of trimming their clothing and moccasins. In a very short time the Indians all over the Plains began using beads to make the same kinds of designs that they had been making with paints and quills. Beadwork soon became such a popular craft among the Plains Indians that many people today speak of "Indian beadwork," as if no other people had ever made any.

In every Plains Indian tribe, though, there were always a few people who kept on using earth paints and porcupine quills. So it happens that when the last war came and the glass beads could not be imported, the Indians still knew how to make their useful things look beautiful.

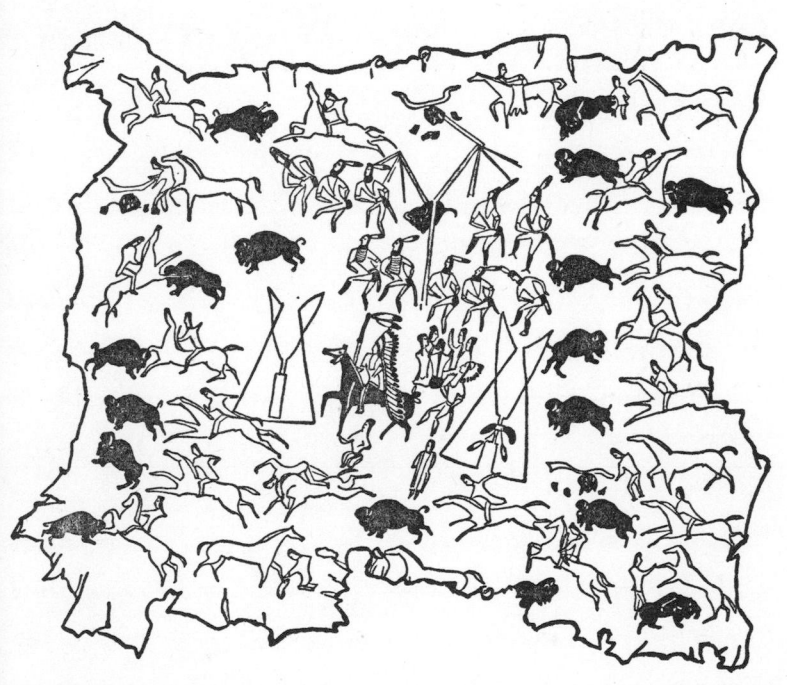

10

WHAT THE PLAINS INDIANS ARE DOING NOW

NOWADAYS, when you go into the Great Plains, you see a farming country that is so rich and famous that sometimes it is called "the Bread-Basket of the World." The land still rolls and ripples like an ocean, but as time goes on the surface of the plains is becoming smoother. That is because men plow the earth and work with it. They, like wind and water, wear away the soil and change the form of the earth.

Where the two great buffalo herds grazed in times past, cattle are grazing now. Where the wild grass once grew "knee high to a man on a horse," wheat and oats and rye now grow as richly. The country that was open to the skyline is fenced in, now, and the roads make straight lines across it. No man may ride across the plains as he pleases today; the roads are there to show him where he may go without doing any damage to the crops, and the land is fenced in to hold him to the lines of the roads.

Every farm on the plains has its house and barn and chicken coops, and at first sight all the farms look alike. If you come closer, though, you may see a house with a brush shelter built in the back yard. You may even find, in a pasture near the house, that a teepee is still standing. Then you know that you have found a Plains Indian home. The Indians still live out of doors in their brush shelters during the summers, and some of the very oldest people like to live in teepees all the year round. There they can sit and remember the buffalo days.

And, if you go into the plains country in summer, you may read in one of the newspapers that are printed there, or hear announced over the radio, the news that an Indian celebration is to be given. If you want to go to the celebration, you must drive over the straight paved roads for a long way. Then you turn off onto a dirt side road that leads back through a cow pasture, to a creek. There, hidden away from people who are not willing to take the trouble to hunt for it, you may see a Sun Dance given. But you will see that the dance and the Indians, like the country, have changed in some ways.

For instead of a circle of buffalo-hide teepees, you will

find a circle of canvas tents, or of trailers. There will be only a few horses tied near the Sun Dance camp, now, though many cars will be parked there. Nowadays, the dance usually lasts only two or three days, instead of eight, and very few men even hope that they will be lucky enough to see visions in the dance. Still the men dance, believing that it is right for them to thank the Power that made the earth for the good things upon it.

Nobody eats buffalo or deer meat, or wild fruits and roots in an Indian camp now. Instead, the people eat beefsteak, and bread from the grocery store, and canned fruits, and the children drink milk. The Plains Indians do not go hunting for food any more. Instead they work, like everybody else, to earn the money with which they buy their food. They do not receive any more help or money from the government than other farmers in the plains country do.

They are good farmers, the Plains Indians, and good stock raisers. Sometimes an Indian boy raises the best calf in his county, and once one of them raised the best calf in his state. Indian girls have won the contests in cooking and canning and dressmaking at state and county fairs. In some states the Indian children go to school with

The Old and the New

the white children, while in others they go to their own special schools.

Besides keeping up their dances and some parts of their old religious beliefs, the Plains Indians have kept some other things that they had in the old days. Most of them, even the younger people, still speak their own tribal languages as well as English. The Indians still remember the songs of the old days, and sing them at home when they are working or resting. Every Plains Indian has an Indian name as well as an English one. Every child knows the history of his tribe, as his grandfather has told it to him, and he is proud of the people who made the tribal history, and proud that he belongs to them.

Most of all, the Plains Indian men are still soldiers. They fought well and hard in the last war. Many of them were paratroopers, and asked to be allowed to fight with the sky troops because that was the most dangerous place to be. Some Indians were fighter pilots, and there were many Plains Indians who were military police, just as the members of the soldier societies were the camp police in the old days. The Army Signal Corps used a Plains Indian language as a code in sending messages. All the specially trained radio operators who used the code were members of one Plains tribe.

Some of the Indian soldiers were killed in the war, and their families mourned for them as if they had been killed on raids in the old days. Many more of the Indian soldiers came home when the fighting was finished, and their families held victory dances and give-aways for them, just as Plains Indians had always done. There were Indian girls who were WACS or WAVES or Army or Navy nurses, and their people were as proud of the girls as they were of the men who went away to fight.

The best thing to say would be that these first Americans are trying hard, now, to be like other Americans. The things that they are keeping from their old way of life are the things that any people would be proud of, and would try to keep. We know how proud they must be, for one of the surest signs that a white man is great in the plains is for him to be adopted into an Indian tribe. No white man who deserves it ever takes that honor lightly.

So, in spite of the changes that time has brought about, the Plains Indians are still the Plains Indians. They are not to be confused with any other Indians, or with any other people in the world.

ACKNOWLEDGMENTS

FOR MATERIAL USED IN PREPARATION OF

ILLUSTRATIONS

The American Museum of Natural History, New York City.

The Chicago Museum of Natural History, Chicago, Illinois.

The Denver Art Museum, Denver, Colorado.

F. H. Douglas, Denver, Colorado.

The Museum of New Mexico, Santa Fe, New Mexico.

The Oklahoma Historical Society, Oklahoma City, Oklahoma.

The United States National Museum (Smithsonian Institution), Washington, D.C.

Miss Amelia Elizabeth White, Santa Fe, New Mexico.

BIBLIOGRAPHY FOR ILLUSTRATIONS

Catlin, G. *North American Indians*. Eighth edition.

Denver Art Museum. Material Culture Notes Series.

D'Harnoncourt, R., and F. H. Douglas. *Indian Art of the United States*.

Dorsey, G. A. *The Cheyenne*.

Ewers, J. C. *Plains Indian Painting*.

Hodge, F. W. *Handbook of American Indians North of Mexico*. Report of the Bureau of American Ethnology, No. 30.

Holling, H. C. *The Book of Indians*.

Lowie, Robert H. *The Crow Indians*.

Lyford, C. A. *Quill and Beadwork of the Western Sioux*.

McKenny, J., and Wm. Hall. *Indians of North America*.

Mallory, G. *Indian Sign Language*. Report of the Bureau of American Ethnology, No. 1.

Marriott, A. *The Ten Grandmothers*.

Mooney, Jas. *The Kiowa Calendar System*. Report of the Bureau of American Ethnology, No. 17, Pt. 1.

Salomon, J. H. *The Book of Indian Crafts and Indian Lore*.

U.S. Department of Agriculture, Forest Service. *Handbook of Range Plants*.

Von Wied, Prince Maximillian. *Early Western Travels*.

Wissler, C. *The American Indian*. First edition.

Wissler, C. *Indian Costumes of the United States*.

Wissler, C. *Indians of the Plains*.

INDEX

134